Reflecting on Faith Schools

Profound changes in society, government policy and the political landscape, together with such cataclysmic events as 9/11 and 7/7, have greatly altered perceptions of faith schools in England. Their publicly funded existence at the beginning of the twenty first century causes considerable public debate.

Taking a reflective practice approach, this study – by people working within faith schools and colleges – explores the new and highly controversial issues surrounding these schools in a sophisticated and thoughtful way. Looking at the supposed secularisation of the west (or at least, some parts of it), the nature of the multi-cultural and multi-faith society, the role of women, the spiritual development of children, and most of all, the form that the tolerance of religious diversity should take in liberal societies, this book encourages readers to re-examine their assumptions and to consider faith schools as a positive part of the future of the English schooling system, within a multi-cultural society. Such schools can also be seen as a means by which the emotional resilience of both staff and pupils can be enhanced.

This book was previously published as a special issue of *The International Journal of Children's Spirituality*.

Helen Johnson is Reader in Education and Director of the Centre for Professional Education Research and Consultancy (CPERC) in the School of Education, Kingston University, UK.

Reflecting on Faith Schools

Edited by Helen Johnson

Routledge
Taylor & Francis Group

LONDON AND NEW YORK

First published 2006 by Routledge
2 Park Square, Milton Park, Abingdon, Oxon, OX14 4RN

Simultaneously published in the USA and Canada
by Routledge
270 Madison Ave, New York, NY 10016

Routledge is an imprint of the Taylor & Francis Group, an informa business

© 2006 Taylor & Francis Ltd

Typeset in by Plantin by Genesis Typesetting Ltd, Rochester, Kent
Printed and bound in Great Britain by Antony Rowe Ltd, Chippenham, Wiltshire

British Library Cataloguing in Publication Data
A catalogue record for this book is available from the British Library

Library of Congress Cataloging in Publication Data
A catalog record for this book has been requested

ISBN10 0-415-40046-5
ISBN13 978-0-415-400466

Faith Schools
Editor: Helen Johnson

CONTENTS

Reflecting on faith schools: an exercise in the sociological imagination

The sociological imagination enables its possessor to understand the larger historical scene in terms of its meaning for the inner life and external career of a variety of individuals. (Wright Mills, 1970, p. 11)

Part A: an argument and some evidence

Less than ten years ago, it was possible to remark on the *lack* of opposition to faith schools (or, as they tended to be called then, church schools). Today, faith schools attract an immense amount of attention from within and outside the field of education and in many national contexts. In England, some of this opposition is both very vocal and intense, some is well argued and some makes no attempt at objectivity. What has happened in this intervening period?

Declared government education policy supporting a faith presence in education, parental perception and choice, seemingly contradictory social trends including secularisation, and cataclysmic events, such as September 11 and 7 July, have contributed to a much-changed context in which these schools operate. As noted elsewhere, faith schools are a phenomenon of our times (Johnson, 2000). It is despite and perhaps because of these factors (and others) that such schools are not merely surviving on the margins but are oversubscribed.

Structural issues

First, it is useful to note faith schools as a *structural* phenomenon. As touched upon in various ways in several chapters, the Anglican church school predates the mass schooling system that has developed in England since Forster's Education Act in 1870 opened up elementary education to working-class children. Both the Anglican National Society and the non-conformist churches had provided elementary schools from the early nineteenth century, offering basic literacy and numeracy skills as a *voluntary* activity. The state, which, at this time, had resisted a direct role for itself in education, from the early nineteenth century until the Forster Act, used the voluntary bodies to channel government grants to assist such schooling. In this book about faith schools in England, Marilyn Holness' chapter, 'New wine in old bottles', offers, for those new to the area, a short overview of some of the more significant historical pivotal moments and explores more fully the importance of voluntarism and difference in the structure of the English dual system of schooling. It offers a historical perspective (touching on secularist, political, social and educational arguments). Perhaps more importantly, and hence its position in the final section (Part C) of this book, the chapter goes on to explore the role of faith schools as part of a wider governmental move to emphasise difference and voluntarism in *current* education policy. Such open governmental approval is far from Churchill's express demand of Butler that church schools were a particular can of worms not to be reopened in the epoch-making Education Act of 1944. The settlement of the Education Act of 1902 was to be left undisturbed, but, most of all, *unmentioned*.

But the excitement in the study of the area of faith schools is that it allows some very large contemporary issues to be explored. Some immediately come to mind: the supposed secularisation of the West (especially Europe); the nature of the multicultural and multifaith society; the role of women; and most of all, the form that tolerance of this diversity should take in liberal societies. In the first chapter in Part A, Mike Castelli and Abdullah Trevathan explore some of these questions, using a contemporary English Muslim context. Determined not to shy away from controversial issues, the second chapter is a full-throated attack on faith schools. Roger Marples, in 'Against faith schools', takes a less than accommodating view, arguing passionately for the rights of the individual child for an open future. For this to happen, he argues, students should not be subjected to what he regards as the indoctrination of the faith school experience. He sets out a philosophical argument, in a confidently modernist perspective.

The other chapters in this book ask and explore their own questions: What is this open future? In the development of our spirituality, can we ever ignore our own starting-point? How many skins do we have to shuck off before we *really* are what we are when we interact with others? This exploration is also predicated on the need for an agreement about the nature and perspectives of liberalism, in which liberals are committed to an emphasis on the individual and his/her rights. Interestingly, the philosopher Anthony Appiah (2005) has recently argued for a 'rooted cosmopolitanism' in which attachments to our families, friends, communities and religions are deep enough to matter but unrestricting enough to allow us to 'move on' and grow in our own self-actualising way, in our own chosen context.

Part B: using reflection to find oneself and the big picture

It is a statement of the obvious that what happens in schools—whatever their type— has a significant impact on the development of young people. After all, young people in our schools learn most powerful and perhaps lasting lessons from watching the behaviour of the adults in their schools. Sizer and Sizer put it vividly:

They watch us all the time. The students, that is. They listen to us, sometimes. They learn from all that watching and listening. Be quiet. Don't cheat. Don't lie. Be nice. Don't fight. They attend to us, more than we usually realize. (Sizer & Sizer, 1999, p. xviii; original italics)

Fullan (2002) has identified as part of the head teacher's role, not only building a shared organisational culture but a professional learning community in which knowledge and attitudes are shared and developed. This leads directly to the question: what are the values that schools *should* and *do* promote? Sizer and Sizer (1999, p. 11) sum up the issues for schools and those within them: 'What do we stand for in this place? How is that stance reflected in our routines, activities and rituals? How do we *model*—as institutions and as the people who work within them—that which we most value?' (their italics).

Without being too glib, it can be seen that faith schools have certain 'givens' that give them as institutions and organisations, sometimes a steer, sometimes a directive, in the way they should behave and perform. They know what is expected of them. But what of individual members of staff, whose own religious and moral perspective may not entirely match the position of their school—and their church or faith body? Following Sizer and Sizer, it is clearly important that school staff are aware of the impression that *all* their behaviour makes, from the formal behaviour played out 'rhetorically' in ceremonies in the school hall to the most casual (and perhaps unthinking) comments made in the rush of the school corridor. After all: 'The kids count on our consistency. Few qualities in adults annoy adolescents more than hypocrisy' (Sizer & Sizer, 1999, p. 11).

So whatever the setting, adults within an educational institution have power, sometimes expressed explicitly; sometimes expressing their authority, and even their domination, in more implicit ways. Thus, it is clearly necessary for them to become aware of their own values and construction of identity, for the supposedly 'powerful' individual to go beyond the self in isolation to find the self in reflection and consequent awareness. In this, for example, it is necessary to:

- examine the marginalisation of the Other;
- investigate the 'taken-for-granted';
- and find one's social, moral and spiritual location in the discourses that he/she uses.

Arguing for autobiographical reflection and data

The task and duty to reflect is therefore clearly one in which all adults within the environs of the educational institution must engage. How should this reflection be facilitated, tracked and recorded? Within education research, there is a strong strain of positivist research and so much use of statistics, performance indicators and other components of performativity. It would seem especially relevant in the audit of educational institutions and systems. Once some form of formal educational process is entered, students and staff become participants in a system that has inputs, processes and outputs. This approach with its objective measurement of specified activity can indicate whether or not a system is functioning effectively in accordance with declared criteria. The debate around the particular advantages and disadvantages of qualitative and quantitative approaches is an old one in education research (and elsewhere in the social sciences). More recent arguments have focused on governmental insistence (both in the UK and the USA) for evidence-based policy and practice. Patti Lather (2004, p. 757) sees such an expectation as 'oversimplif[ying] complex problems' and 'as being used to warrant governmental incursion into legislating scientific method'. In particular, she argues that one reading of such a move to evidence-based approaches is to see it as an expression of a 'regressive modernism' that is 'disciplining', 'normalizing' and 'standard[izing]' educational research (Lather, p. 766). The danger in such an approach is that the 'spaces for doing other sorts of research' into the changes in the crumbling, old hegemonies are limited. She goes on to conclude that: 'This backlash attempt to transfer a medical model to educational research might be read as an "assault, direct and indirect, on multiculturalism" (Hall, 1996, p. 468)'.

But what if the task *is* to find out how people feel about what has happened to them, what has been the lasting impact of events and exposure to particular cultures and religious faiths? After all, education, if regarded as a process of personal development, can take place wherever the spirit moves. Thus, as the above discussion has shown, perhaps an approach that seeks richer and thicker data is required to do more than skate across the surface of received and perhaps out-moded realities. An approach that fully embraces qualitative research can offer such a means. Such an interpretative perspective offers 'a process of exploration', in which, according to Hammersley and Atkinson (1983, p. 12): 'the researcher comes face-to-face with social situations that reveal ... constructs and the taken-for-granted components of such worlds'.

These elements can be understood through a holistic understanding or 'mind-map' (Argyris & Schon, 1974), based on interactions between the subject matter and its external context and vice versa. In this task of understanding, we can call up Weber's distinction between the direct observation of the meaning of manifested subject matter (which includes verbalisations or 'verbal utterances'). (This allows a more deep understanding of why the teacher or individual did what she did). Recalling Weber (1978, p. 8), 'This ... consists in placing the act in an intelligible and more inclusive context of meaning'. These two types of understanding, *Erklaren* (explanation) and *Verstehen* (understanding) clearly require different methodologies (Habermas, 1990, p. 10).

While there may be social constructions of reality that are governed by identifiable rules and regulations, no objective patterns of reality exist. Individuals have the capacity to make their own reality and so exercise a choice in deciding to act out this rather than that: 'the acting individual attaches a subjective meaning' (Weber, 1978, p. 24) to his or her own behaviour 'be it overt or covert, omission or acquiescence'. So, in practical terms, whereas quantitative research seeks to measure behaviour, qualitative research attempts to go beneath the surface to explore a deeper understanding of the meanings of a particular situation, as offered by the situational actors themselves.

The collection of data about the individual's history and experiences

It is in this complexity of contextualisation and personal realities, that the experiences of adults within educational institutions as actors making things happen can be reported in various ways. Returning to C. Wright Mills' remark about the link between 'the larger historical scene' and 'the inner life and career of a variety of individuals', Goodson and Sikes (2001, p. 10) take this point and apply it to the field of educational studies:

> Working with teachers ... who are, again, arguably marginal in terms of their social power, life history has been seen as particularly useful and appropriate because, as Bullough (1998, pp. 20–21) points out 'public and private cannot ... be separated ... The person comes through'.

It is *this person* and the construction of identity with which we are concerned. But how unstructured should the autobiography or life history be? Clearly the life history and experience review is being entered into with the expectation that some incidents may be more relevant or meaningful than others.

Trying out the reflective method

The set of life history and experience reviews presented in Part B are concerned with revealing participants' involvement with a particular aspect of faith schools and institutions. Adapting Goodson and Sikes' (2001, p. 30) comments about the use of time-lines to focus reflection, our snowball sample of reviewers has discussed some of the following:

- Place and date of birth
- Family background and birthplace
- Religious background
- Education, preschool experiences, school experience: courses taken, subjects favoured, credentials achieved; general character of school experiences; peer relations; teachers; 'good' and 'bad' experiences
- Education, college/university attended
- Occupation, general work history, changes of job, types of school, types of position.

What is offered in the way of personal reflection, in the manner of life history? A range of methods and reportages is used in Part B's symposium of reflection but all revolve the use of constant *questioning*: the second part of this editorial explores the method more fully. Catherine Hill discusses the impact of trauma on children's well-being in a variety of contexts; Robert Jones discusses the forming of a religious perspective that though Christian is not hegemonic and its impact on his own role as a chaplain in a higher education college with a faith basis; Howard Worsley discusses being an actor in the setting up of a faith school. Lynne Scholefield writes about her travels in two cultures so that one identity can evolve. In pursuit of one individual truth about the impact of being a student at a faith school, an interview with a former faith school student asks some very direct questions and gets some equally direct answers. As ever, there are more questions than answers, and the third part of the editorial attempts some conclusions about the symposium.

Part C: lessons from the international scene and guesses about the future

Many of the issues that arise in the English context are found in other contexts too. Denis McLaughlin, writing from Brisbane, Australia, is concerned with the popularity of fee-paying Catholic schools in a supposedly secularising—and egalitarian—Australia. He offers a historical overview of the development of Catholic schools, linked as it is to the Irish Catholic experience in Australia, and its subordinate position to hegemonic Protestantism. He goes on to report on some robustly positivist research that surveyed the attitudes of students whilst attending Catholic schools. He offers a picture, one feels, that has echoes in the English experience: that Catholic schools have many purposes, both educational and religious; and while those working within them or supporting them may have as their primary concern 'the nurturing of the human community', parents may be more attracted to the 'quality education' provided within them. The issues of social divisiveness and elitism do not go away; but does such separateness automatically mean segregation? What do the students themselves really want in terms of spirituality? Marion Maddox (2005, p. 162) has said of her Australian university students: 'As in other secular, western countries, a personalised, free-form and eclectic spirituality seems to be replacing commitments for and against religion. My students, who dread to be seen as "religious" … are proud to be called to be "spiritual"'.

However these young people define 'spirituality', it may not conform to the expectations of mainstream adult society; and it is clear that 'new forms' of spirituality are emerging. We do not have space here to investigate how free of influences from established religious traditions this new spirituality really is; and, of course, this spirituality can continue to express itself through belief in and living through the more traditional forms of the established religions. Marion Maddox's students can point to 'the wrongs religions have perpetrated', and the case against organised religions is not trivial. However, as Maddox goes on to note:

> Religious traditions carry the collective memory of generations of committed thinkers, trained and lay, devoting themselves to pressing human problems. The trial and error nature of individual, internalised spirituality has attractions, but it leaves every seeker reinventing their own wheel (2005, p. 162).

None, new and old

This argument around the 'old' religious traditions is not going to be settled here; but it is enough to note that the case has not been proven one way or the other and is unlikely to be. It is a matter of belief, emotional need and of choice. All we can do, in fairness, is to examine our *automatic* positions and how they might impact on how we regard ourselves and others. One important assumption that has direct significance to this discussion is the acceptance that our society is increasingly becoming secularised.

That may or may not be the general case; however, it is clear that many students within education come from families and communities that live within active religious traditions. It is likely that the latter will influence, to a greater or lesser degree, how they express their life perspective and needs—as much as secularism or disbelief or 'new' 'unattached' spiritualities will influence their fellow students. So we arrive at a mixture. It is this—these families and communities and, most importantly, others of different faiths and none—that is served by faith schools.

Helen Johnson
Reader in Education
School of Education, Kingston University, UK

References

Appiah, K. A. (2005) *The ethics of identity* (Princeton, NJ, Princeton University Press).

Argyris, C. & Schon, D. (1974) *Theory in practice: increasing professional effectiveness* (Harmondsworth, Penguin).

Bullough, R. (1998) *First year teacher* (New York, Teachers College Press).

Fullan, M. (2002) The role of leadership in the promotion of knowledge management in schools, *Teachers and Teaching*, 8(4), 409–420.

Goodson, I. & Sikes, P. (2001) *Life history research in educational settings: learning from lives* (Buckingham, Open University Press).

Habermas, J. (1990) *Moral Consciousness and Communitive Action*, translated by C. Lenhardt & S. Weber Nicholsen (Cambridge, Polity).

Hall, S. (1996) quoted in D. Morley & K.-H. Chen (Eds) *Stuart Hall: critical dialogues in cultural studies* (London, Routledge).

Hammersley, M. & Atkinson, E. (1983) *Ethnography: principles in practice* (London, Routledge).

Johnson, H. (2000) Surviving and thriving in a secularized culture: the phenomenon of religious (church/faith) schools in England, *Journal of Research on Christian Education*, 9(1), 115–135.

Lather, P. (2004) Scientific research in education: a critical perspective, *British Educational Research Journal*, 30(6), 759–772.

Maddox, M. (2005) *God under Howard: the rise of the religious right in Australian politics* (Crows Nest, Allen & Unwin).

Mills Wright, C. (1970) *The sociological imagination* (Harmondsworth, Pelican).

Sizer, T. R. & Sizer, N. F. (1999) *The students are watching: schools and the moral contract* (Boston, MA, Beacon Press).

Weber, M. (1978) *Economy and society: an outline of interpretative sociology* (original work published 1921) (Berkeley, CA, University of California Press).

PART A: AN ARGUMENT

The English public space: developing spirituality in English Muslim schools

Mike Castelli and Abdullah Trevathan

> Go travel the world, watch, look for the truth and the secret of life—every road will lead
> you to this sense of initiation: the light, the secret, are hidden in the place from which you
> set out. You are on your way not toward the end of the road but toward its beginning; to
> go is to return; to find is to rediscover. Go! ... you will return. (Ramadan, 2004, p. VII)

There are at present five Muslim schools within the English state education system
(Open Society Institute, 2005). They have joined Christian, Jewish and one Sikh
school in a dual system of faith community and secular state schools that constitute
English state education. All state schools are commissioned 'to promote pupils' spiritual, moral, social and cultural development' (HMSO, 1988) and a later Act
(HMSO, 1992) ensures that they are inspected by the Office for Standards in Education (Ofsted) on their response to this commission. The children and the families that
form these schools, both faith community and secular, live, grow and learn in a
contemporary English society that is shaped by a secular, post-modern context. How
schools deliver children's spiritual development in this context continues to raise
epistemological and methodological issues. The question of whether spirituality can

be taught in a post-modern, secular society, and if so, how, faces schools and faith communities alike. One school of thought would claim that spirituality can only take place within the context of a faith tradition (Cole, 1990; Thatcher, 1999), others, that spirituality is an innate human quality independent of a given faith position (Hay and Nye, 1998), and others again, that unless there is agreement on the nature of spirituality, it is unrealistic, not to say unfair, to expect schools to undertake the task of spiritual development.

For the contemporary children's spirituality in a Muslim state school society post-modern and secular are two among a range of issues confronting a multifarious English Muslim community. Their task is to develop a coherent Islam that brings together experiences rooted in a myriad of communities and cultures from across the globe. Young English Muslims, in this global community, face the same experiences as other young people in English society and a contemporary, coherent Islam seeks to find spirituality and a language that speaks to this. The process of finding a current language of spirituality is a challenge the Muslim community shares with other faith communities which also wish to help their children and young people grow and flourish in western society. It is indeed the challenge faced by any education community that wishes to take children's spiritual development seriously. The discourse that arises in this common search is a creative, critical dialogue with a larger English society in which not only is the nature of spiritual development at issue, but also the nature of English education and the nature of English society itself. How to be Muslim and English, or Jewish and English or Anglican, Catholic, agnostic, or atheist, in a twenty-first-century England is a challenge whose consequences reach beyond the religious education lesson, and beyond the school as a whole, to a larger English society that is faced with questions of identity from young Muslims, Jews, Anglicans, Catholic, agnostics and atheists in their search for their place in today's England.

The Education Reform Act of 1988 has put spirituality firmly on today's education agenda and the search for a language of discourse to date has been largely a Christian-post-modernist dialogue. Seeking a language which moves the discourse beyond this paradigm to include other faith positions is a further challenge. The language of contextual theology may meet this challenge as it seeks ways of communicating with the contemporary and everyday yet remaining faithful to the Christian tradition. It is the proposition of this chapter that the contextual theological discourses of liberation, ecology and feminism offer the opportunity of addressing issues that are relevant to society and are a challenge to both Islam and Christianity. As Christianity and Islam grapple with these contemporary challenges they may well find themselves not only in dialogue with contemporary society but also with each other.

Typologies for spirituality

Mary Grey (1999) suggests that the three typologies of liberation, ecology and feminism offer the possibility of a spirituality that is relevant to the contemporary classroom. Grey sets these typologies firmly within a Christian context. However, when extended to a Muslim context they offer a challenge to both the Muslim and the larger education communities.

Liberation theology, according to Grey, can speak to contemporary society from two major perspectives. First, its methodology challenges the supremacist model of theology, politics and cultural influence: 'The very success of the supremacist logic of domination/subjugation depends on not hearing anything other than the prevailing patterns of reasoning and content of argument' (1999, p. 18). Second, liberation theology's methodology of remembering the community's story roots the present in a community experience that reaches back as it looks forward:

> All the theologies of liberation, each in its own unique way, base their theological reflection on story, narrative, recovery of narratives obscured or destroyed by oppressive regimes and so on. Hence, resisting domination is at the same time engaging responsibly with tradition. (1999, p. 19)

Grey points out that in an ecological theology this world is our home and the place of revelation of the divine. An ecological spirituality poses epistemological and philosophical questions as it challenges our ways of perceiving and knowing the world. It opposes the dominant oppositional dualism of the humanity/nature, man/animal, body/mind paradigms (1999, p. 21).

Feminist theology consistently crosses the boundary between theory and practice, resists simplistic categorisation, is consistently trying to maintain relationship while respecting and celebrating difference, and maintains a hermeneutic of suspicion in the face of all dominant strands of the intellectual western tradition. Consequently, Grey (p. 22) argues, feminist theology offers a paradigm for all liberations theologies, exposing the blindness or one-sided approach of many of our western traditions.

Young Muslims hear and participate in 'the prevailing patterns of reasoning and content of argument' of contemporary English society and are necessarily influenced by these. The values of materialism, consumerism and individualism are paraded before Muslim children, as they are before all children in western society. The choice for the Muslim community, when raising their children in this context, is either to try and isolate their children from contemporary influences, and success in this is not assured, or to listen to their children's experiences, understand and respect these experiences and, through dialogue, to explore a Muslim spirituality that responds to them. The challenge for the sympathetic non-Muslim, including the teacher, is to listen to, and hear, the Muslim community's experience of this undertaking, recognising that they are not alone in seeking a spirituality that will match the task.

Islam and the West

Shadid and von Konigsveld (1991) identify three factors shaping contemporary western Islam as it seeks to find its place in society. First, 'the partial transplantation of a cultural-religious heritage' in which the struggle to preserve the past meets the need to live in the present. Second, 'the partial blending of religions variants caused by inter-group contacts', in which not only does an Asian meet an African and western Islam but, and, this is their third point, here they meet Christianity, Hinduism,

Sikhism, Judaism, Buddhism and all the other faith and secular communities seeking a contemporary relevance in a post-modern West. It is no surprise, therefore, that within the English Muslim community many different cultural and theological positions are merging from the different Muslim homelands. The predominance of an Islamic cultural heritage from the Indian sub-continent emerging from the *Hanafi* school of thought, alongside the influence of the Ottoman Empire, embodies a more prescriptive paradigm of religious and spiritual matters. The more existential and fluid *Maliki* school of thought represented by the North African communities is making its presence felt in the large urban centres and increasingly adopted by young educated Asians of Pakistani and Indian backgrounds. The phenomenon of large groups of young British Muslims studying in Syria introduces a note of traditional scholasticism through the more legalistic approach of the *Shafi* school of thought. This engagement with an international, pluriform Islam is a search by young Muslims in the West for an Islam that is faithful to the tradition and speaks to the contemporary experience.

> We are currently living through a veritable silent revolution in Muslim communities in the West: more and more young people and intellectuals are actively looking for a way to live in harmony with their faith while participating in the societies that are their societies, whether they like it or not. (Ramada, 2004, p. 4)

But not all Muslims accept the need for change and the fault lines of this disagreement lie around the understanding of the Islamic message in relation to the exoteric and the esoteric; the legalistic and the visual, concerned with external observance and the keeping of the letter of the law, and the spiritual and symbolic, concerned with living from conviction and less for external form. In broader terms, this is the intellectual tradition opposed to the purely legalistic tradition. 'Modern controversies among Muslims, such as the debate over sunna ... should be viewed as skirmishes in an ongoing battle between tradition and modernity, revelation and reason, liberalism and reaction' (Brown, 1996, p. 2).

What differentiates the intellectual tradition from the legalistic approach of Islamic law *(shariah)* is its concern with the 'why' of things rather than the 'how'. The legalists tend to concern themselves largely with telling people what they must do, whereas the intellectual tradition asks questions concerning the fundamental nature of things within the matrix of ultimate reality. While the religious law is essential to the Muslim existence, it is built upon principles that transcend it. The intellectual tradition has always concentrated on these principles *(usul ul fiqh)*, and by clarifying them, applies them in ways appropriate to each situation without breaking either the spirit or the letter of *sharia*. For over a century this intellectual tradition has been somewhat eclipsed by legalist and modernist perspectives and what occurs is that, without the knowledge of the principles, contemporary approaches can be advanced to observe a *sharia* that is separated from the spirit of the law in a way that does not seek to explain its meaning and spirit to young people or to anyone else. This is not helpful to young Muslims growing up in a society where laws have to be justified and unacceptable laws challenged.

Tradition and change

There had traditionally been a balance within Islam between two theological perspectives on the nature of God, namely *tanzih* (incomparability) and *tashbih* (immanence). Those theologians who have had an almost exclusive emphasis on God's incomparability are usually the more dogmatic and exoteric. From this position, God is inaccessible and beyond all understanding. God is a reality far beyond human concerns. This is a God who is distantly other. At the same time the *tashbih* perspective points to a more familiar God, one who is involved in the everyday affairs of the world, aware and responsive and, in this respect, is a personal God who is the other seeking dialogue. Teachers who lay undue emphasis on the outward and legal teachings of Islam focus upon God's incomparability. This is a wrathful God and therefore believers must be warned of hell and divine punishment. Those more concerned with the spiritual dimension lay stress on the prophetic saying; 'God's mercy precedes His wrath'; the first position stresses God's incomparability, distance and otherness; the second, God's familiarity, nearness and sameness. Generally the two positions have coexisted throughout Islamic history yet there has been an increasing tendency over the last 200 years towards the authoritarian *tanzih* theology coinciding with the slow demise of the Ottoman Empire and the colonial conquest of the Muslim world. In this present age, the aim of the Muslim community should be to regain the balance between these two perspectives which is *tawhid*, the absolute unity and inter-relatedness of all reality from which grows a spirituality that can bring an Islamic dimension to liberation, ecological and feminist typologies.

Liberation spirituality

Liberation theology's methodological challenge to what Grey calls 'supremacist domination' speaks to both the Muslim community and the contemporary English community. A relevant English Islam will not be achieved through the domination of one cultural–religious heritage or theology but by a rich blending of traditions that can speak to young Muslims as they seek their place in English society. *Tajdeed* (renewal) is the process of remaining true to the tradition but seeking ways to change so that the tradition can speak to the contemporary. For the larger English society, the supremacist domination of any one English culture over others in the twenty-first century is counter to an English tradition of hospitality and integration that stretches back over centuries and successfully accepted thousands of Jews fleeing Tsarist persecution in the eighteenth and nineteenth centuries (Gartner, 1973, p.231; Valins *et al.*, 2001, p. 7) or Catholics fleeing an Irish famine in the nineteenth century (Hickman, 1995).

Muslims living in the West, and assuming a rightful role within the public sphere, need a language that can be understood and has something to say. Remembering the classical balance between *tashbih* and *tanzih* is part of the educative task that recognises *tajdeed* is not change for the sake of change or change to meet the transient demands of a consumer society, but a renewing of what is best within the tradition while remaining faithful to the indispensable. Telling the whole story of the tradition and remembering the richness and diversity of that narrative is a communal activity. As Grey states:

> it is difficult to overemphasise the importance of remembering as a communal activity and as a counter-cultural contrast to society's excessive individualism ... The way the primary memory of spiritual vision can be recalled to develop a more mature spirituality in adulthood has long been recognised ... the attempt to integrate the theological theme of remembering as communal tasks confronts the inadequacy of the present narrow view of the 'subject' through insisting that any textual study must be rooted in communication praxis. (1999, p. 19)

Within a school context this inclusive response to the religious and cultural experiences of adults and children will be both formative and normative and part of a continuous narration of a living tradition in which young people are invited to be and feel partners. As young people develop their spiritual autobiography, they engage with the community story in a manner that challenges and/or confirms their own life experiences and stories. The adult, the teacher, as guide and fellow pilgrim, listens, and hearing the young person's own stories, recognises the challenges they face in contemporary English society as young Muslims as they face a complex range of cultural, societal, moral and religious influences and identities.

Ecospirituality

Classical Islam expresses its relationship with the environment in architecture, design and nature and understands these as spiritual loci for engaging with the creative presence of God. While exploring the theology of creation within a Classical Islam the contemporary issues associated with ecology and environmental concerns coincide. This combination of theology and contemporary social, political and ecological issues offers the opportunity for the Muslim community to engage young Muslims in a Classical Islam that speaks to contemporary society and its concerns in a spirituality that is Islamic and addresses pressing world concerns.

> Khalifa—or the role of stewardship—is the sacred duty God has ascribed to the human race. There are many verses in the Qur'an that describe human duties and responsibilities, such as the following which aptly summarizes humanity's role: 'It is God who has appointed you viceroys in the earth' (6: 165.) Humankind has a special place in God's scheme. We are more than friends of the earth—we are its guardians. Although we are equal partners with everything else in the natural world we have added responsibilities. We are decidedly not its lords and masters (Khalid, 1996, p. 2).

The care of the environment is one of the major ethical issues facing the twenty-first century for all peoples, and Islam has something to say on this that is challenging and relevant for both the Muslim and wider societies. Developing a relationship with the environment where care and responsibility grow out of wonder and awe is a spirituality that finds resonance in the classroom. For faith communities the task is:

> the work of constructing an aesthetic theology, a theology of beauty based concretely on eco-justice ... a theology reaching beyond the bounds of the religions, in dialogue with

poets, artists and musicians from many cultures and traditions ... a theology of culture which is focused on the celebration, joy and creativity. (Grey, 1999, p. 24)

Feminism and spirituality

Women's issues are now an integral part of modern Islamic discourses, as evidenced in the plethora of 'Women and Islam' titles in religious publishing projects all over the Muslim world. In practice, this has entailed re-reading of the old texts in search of solutions—or more precisely, Islamic alternatives—for a very modern problem, which has to do with the changed status of women and the need to accommodate their aspirations for equality and to define and control their increasing participation in the politics of the Muslim world. (Mir-Hosseini, 1996, p. 285)

Feminist theology offers a paradigm for contemporary Islam on two counts. First, it challenges the 'dominant strands of the intellectual Western tradition' (Grey, 1999, p. 21) and also challenges the western, and some Muslim, misinterpretations of the place of women in society in general and within Islam in particular (Badran, 2001; Barlas, 2002). Young Muslim men and women are growing up in a society where equality and inclusion is a gender as well as a race and cultural issue. Developing a spirituality in which feminism offers a typology relevant for both Muslim and non-Muslim, male and female alike, is likely to provoke reactions from many sides. The task in the classroom is to use these reactions as moments of reflection, as opportunities for an examination of the cause of these reactions in a manner that can lead young people to look inwards but also to raise their sights beyond themselves.

Our task ... is to take the most transparent, the most symbolic, of the concerns of our pupils, in the hope that they will be led from the trivial and immediate and the local to the significant, the enduring, and the universal concern. (Hull, 1984, p. 13)

Dialogue

When faith community schools argue that religious education takes place at two inter-connected levels within their schools they cite curriculum religious education and a religious education that permeates the whole of the life of the school (Catholic Education Service, 1999; Bailey, 2002). In a similar fashion, we wish to suggest, the three theological and spiritual typologies discussed in this chapter could permeate the whole curriculum in any school. Liberation has as much to do with English literature or physical education, and ecology, science or geography, and feminism, maths or music, as any of them has to do with religious education. In this range of contexts, they pose epistemological and philosophical questions which challenge our ways of perceiving and knowing the world. Furthermore, the language of liberation is different, yet complementary, in Bolton and Bogotá, that of ecology in Manhattan and Mumbai, and a feminist reading of Ad Tuendam Fidem (John Paul II, 1998) will not be that of the author himself. Within each context confronting these issues can be spiritual education in Hull's terms.

> We must reject the idea that the spiritual is a separable part of the human. Someone might think that when the education law refers to spiritual, moral and cultural, that these are part of being human. It is better, however, to regard these as aspects or dimensions of the human rather than as parts or sections … The spiritual refers to the way we realise the potential of our biological nature by transcending previous levels. (Hull, 2002, p. 172)

These opportunities for spiritual education within a Muslim, Christian, Jewish, Sikh, Buddhist, Hindu or secular setting offer opportunities for dialogue between spiritualities within a contemporary educational context. Within a Muslim faith community school context, they can not only speak faithfully to the tradition but also allow that tradition to speak to contemporary society with a Muslim voice, in a language and a spirituality that is both Muslim and English. Anyone approaching issues of liberation, ecology or feminism with an open mind, open heart and a willingness to change could find opportunities for dialogue in an English public space that is inclusive, empowering and relevant for a twenty-first-century English education system concerned with children's spiritual development.

Notes on contributors

Mike Castelli is Principal Lecturer in Education at Roehampton University, UK.
Abdullah Trevathan is a Research Fellow at Roehampton University UK and is head teacher of the Islamia Primary School, in North London, UK.

References

Badran, M. (2001) Understanding Islam, Islamism, and Islamic feminism, *Journal of Women's History*, 13(1), 452–476.
Bailey, J. (2002) Religious education in church schools, in: Broadbent, L. & Brown, A. (Eds) *Issues in religious education* (London, RoutledgeFalmer).
Barlas, A. (2002) *'Believing women in Islam'; unreading patriarchal interpretations of the Qur'an* (Austin, TX, University of Texas Press).
Brown, D. (1996) *Rethinking tradition in modern Islamic thought* (Cambridge, Cambridge University Press).
Catholic Education Service (CES) (1999) *Evaluating the distinctive nature of Catholic schools* (London, CES).
Cole, R. (1990) *The spiritual life of children* (London, Harper Collins).
Garther, L. (1973) *The Jewish Immigration in England 1870–1914* (London, Simon Publications).
Grey, M. (1999) in: Thatche, A. (ed) *Spirituality and the Curriculum* (London, Cassells).
Hay, D. & Nye, R. (1998) *The spirit of the child* (London, Harper Collins).
Hickman, M. (1995) *Religion, class and identity: the state, the Catholic Church and the education of the Irish in Britain* (Aldershot, Avebury).
HMSO (1988) *The Education Reform Act* (London, HMSO).
HMSO (1992) *Education (schools) Act* (London, HMSO).
Hull, J. M. (Ed.) (1984) *Studies in religion and education* (Lewes, Falmer).
Hull, M. J. (2002) Spiritual development: interpretations and applications, *British Journal of Religious Education*, 24(3), 171–182.
John Paul III (May, 1998) *Ad Tvendam Fidem*, Rome, Congregation for the Defence of the Faith.
Khalid F. (1996) Guardian of the planet, *Ourplanet*, 8(2). Available online at: www.ourplanet.com
Lewis, P. (1994) *Islamic Britain* (London, Tuaris & Co).

Mir-Hosseini, Z. (1996) Stretching the limits: a feminist reading of the shari'a in post-Khomeini Iran, in: M. Yamani (Ed.) *Feminism and Islam* (London, Ithaca Press).

Open Society Institute (OSI) (2005) *Muslims in the UK; policies for engaged citizens* (New York, OSI).

Ramadan, T. (2004) *Western Muslims and the future of Islam* (Oxford, OUP).

Shadid, W. A. R. & Von Koningsveld, P. S. (1991) *The integration of Islam and Hinduism in western Europe* (Kampen, Kok Pharos Publishing House).

Thatcher, A. (1999) *Spirituality and the curriculum* (London, Cassell).

Valins, O. *et al* (2001) *The future of Jewish schools in the United Kingdom* (London, Institute of Jewish Policy Research).

Against faith schools: a philosophical argument for children's rights

Roger Marples

Introduction

If it were not for the Church of England, through the Anglican and National Society and the non-conformist British and Foreign School Society's concern for elementary schooling in England in the early years of the nineteenth century, there would, in all probability, have been little in the way of formal education for the vast majority of children before 1870. Since then the number of Church schools, including Roman Catholic schools, has continued to grow with approximately one in three of the nation's children attending state-funded faith schools. During the twentieth century Britain was transformed into a multifaith and multi-ethnic society while at the same time becoming a largely secular society.[1] Church schools today are therefore in a remarkably privileged position.

In 2001, as part of its concern for diversity of educational provision, the British government proposed that religious minorities should be encouraged to open their own faith schools, for which there would be state funding (DfEE, 2001). It is all too easy to welcome this decision with cries of 'About time too!' but there is another equally valid and equally consistent response, and that is to abolish all schools with a religious foundation. I shall argue that this is the most appropriate course of action for a liberal democracy to take.

Every society has a legitimate interest in the kind of education its young people receive. What happens to children in school, in terms of the curriculum content and the teaching they receive, has a major causal role in affecting the kind of society in which we all live. A system of schooling may be designed for many reasons, not all of which are morally acceptable. Children have been forced to attend schools whose specific intentions included producing Christian gentlemen or committed communists, where any reference to the potentially liberating possibilities afforded by schooling have met with incomprehension or hostility. Those who have wished to indoctrinate the young into particular conceptions of the good life have all too frequently found schools willing to accommodate them. Part of what is involved in assessing the moral acceptability of a system of schooling is the extent to which children are manipulated or controlled for purposes other than those they would freely endorse. If teachers were indifferent to children possessing relevant information as well as the ability to critically evaluate it, they would be in breach of their moral responsibilities towards them. But children also have lives beyond school, as children and as adult citizens. They will have to relate to countless other people and institutions, and it is for this reason that the wider society of which they are a part has a stake in the kind of education they receive.

Parental rights

Those of us who wish to abolish faith schools are frequently accused of being in breach of the Universal Declaration of Human Rights, whereby parents have the right 'to ensure (an) education and teaching in conformity with their own religious and philosophical convictions'. Before exploring the extent to which faith schools might be incompatible with the legitimate interests of children and the society of which they are members, I hope to be able to demonstrate that the argument for faith schools by reference to parental rights is far weaker than its defenders would have us believe.

The view that children are little more than parental property continues to be widely held. Charles Fried, for example, argues that the right to form one's child's life plan is an extension of the basic right not to be interfered with (Fried, 1978, p. 152). More recently Robert Nozick has suggested that children are part of the parent's 'substance' in the same way that they are part of a parent's 'wider identity' (Nozick, 1989, p. 28). It goes without saying that (most) parents conceive of their parental status as part of their personal identity and find parenthood to be a source of profound satisfaction and fulfilment. But it is one thing to recognise this and quite another to conclude that it provides sufficient justification for the claim that the *interests* of parents and children are coincidental and harmonious, or that simply in virtue of occupying the role of parent, one is optimally equipped to determine a child's best interests. A child has interests in being able to formulate her own values and life plans and this is true whether or not she happens to be interested *in* any such thing. This is why Fried, in seeing a child as a mere extension of her parent with an 'identity between chooser and chosen for' (1978, p. 152), is so far off the mark in refusing to acknowledge the extent to which the interests of parents and children may so frequently fail to converge. If children are mere appendages of their parents, their moral status as independent persons is both disrespected and undermined.

It would be foolish to underestimate the extent to which the argument from parental extension is invoked in discussions of so-called parental rights to faith schools, especially when it is couched in the more appealing language of familial intimacy. According to Ferdinand Schoeman (1980, p. 6):

> it is the significance of intimacy, and not just a concern for the best interests of the child, that is essential to understanding the basis of the parents' moral claim to raise their biological offspring in a context of privacy, autonomy and responsibility.

While it would be absurd to deny the value of intimate relationships within the context of family life or to resist temptations on the part of non-family members to interfere, it is questionable whether the value attributed to such relationships can be cashed out in the language of *rights* without losing much of the importance we properly attribute to them. If parents do have the right to mould their children in accordance with their own religious convictions, then an argument with considerably more justificatory force than appeal to the value of intimate relationships is called for. It is impossible to imagine meaningful parent–child relationships in which children were not brought up to share their parents' enthusiasms, including the importance parents might attach to family prayers. None of this lends support to the notion of a parental *right* to mould a child as if she were a miniature version of themselves. The error here, as David Archard recognises, is the belief that children are no more than 'instruments' of their parents' good (Archard, 2002, p. 151). The fact that so many people regard the begetting and rearing of children as indispensable to their own well-being—a form of flourishing which may well be conceived less in terms of self-gratification than a concern for the best interests of the child—does nothing to show that parents qua parents have any rights at all. Philip Montague has gone so far as to argue that the very idea of parental rights is a myth. At the heart of the parent–child relationship, he says, are responsibilities or obligations that parents have to protect the interests of their children and to nurture the children's decision-making abilities. Such obligations are child-centred rather than parent-centred 'because of the orientation all rights have towards their possessors' (Montague, 2000, p. 57). If there were such things as parental rights it would follow, Montague argues, that parents would have discretion over whether or not to protect their children's welfare—something which is clearly incompatible with the existence of parental obligations (Montague, 2000, p. 62). All of which, he concludes, is perfectly compatible with allowing a measure of latitude in *how* parents might care for their children; discretion regarding how to fulfil one's obligations being very different from discretion over what is to *count* as fulfilling them. The granting of discretionary powers to parents would thereby limit the extent to which outside agencies should be permitted to interfere with parents' decision-making relating to their children's welfare, while at the same time denying that parents have a right to implement such decisions.[2]

Several recent writers have invoked the idea of parent as 'trustee' and characterised the parent–child relationship as a form of fiduciary relationship in attempts to find an appropriate justification for parental authority.[3] The plausibility of such a view rests on the assumption that children are not autonomous and, in important respects, are lacking in moral agency. To the extent that reference to rights is appropriate in the context of child-rearing, it is the child's right 'in trust' to become an autonomous moral agent and to what Joel Feinberg so memorably refers to as an 'open future' (Feinberg, 1970), where significant options in life—such as one's religion—are not foreclosed. This is an appealing notion for several reasons. Not only is it a realistic and hard-edged view about children and the conditions required for autonomous well-being, it is resistant to the idea of children's rights carrying more weight than it merits. One of the major concerns shared by those of us with strong reservations about faith schools is that they may not attach sufficient importance to children's autonomy. Before exploring this further, it is important see what it is about children that gives them rights 'in trust' as opposed to rights per se.

Children's rights

James Griffin (Griffin, 2002) and Harry Brighouse (Brighouse, 2002) are particularly illuminating in what they have to say about children's rights. Brighouse usefully distinguishes between 'welfare' and 'agency' rights. While acknowledging that children might appropriately be said to be the bearers of welfare rights (to education, for example) they are both sceptical about attributing agency to them on the grounds that they—or at least younger members of that class—are lacking the appropriate wherewithal for competent (or autonomous) choice. Brighouse is persuasive in demonstrating that in three significant and relevant respects children are, for the most part, different from adults in being heavily dependent on others for their well-being, highly vulnerable to the decisions of others and, unlike other people who are dependent and vulnerable, have the capacity to develop the capabilities to meet their own needs. As such they differ from the senile, the mentally retarded and domestic pets.[4] These distinguishing features of children render them unique and, as Griffin says, it is their potential agency combined with their vulnerability which is in large part responsible for the especially strong obligations we feel towards them (p. 27), while according to Brighouse it is the key notions of 'competence' and 'rationality' which are the prerequisites for proper attribution of agency rights. Brighouse is sensitive to the difficulties of specifying the time in a child's life when the competence threshold is realised above which it is appropriate to grant agency rights. However, until we have a measure of confidence that it has been crossed, it would be foolhardy to grant children agency rights appropriate to sane adults even if it is incumbent upon parents and agencies of the state, such as schools, to provide them with opportunities for agency. Robert Noggle is at pains to emphasise that the competence threshold requires rather more than merely cognitive competence but includes a well-developed capacity for *moral* agency. Until children have developed fairly stable preference structures and are capable of evaluative judgements required for effective interaction with other moral agents, they lack what he calls 'temporally extended agency' and, as such, are incapable of identifying with their future selves (Noggle, 2002, p. 101). Lacking the cognitive and conceptual apparatus with which to evaluate and endorse the values and beliefs which govern their lives, children are only 'prospective or probationary members of the moral community' (p.100). In the meantime it is the responsibility of the parent to ensure that the child develops the appropriate skills and capacities with the parental role gradually shifting from a directive to a veto role.

Open future

It is the child's right to an open future on which I now wish to focus. It will not only provide a sharper focus to the nature of parental obligations, but it will serve to provide limitations by reference to which the actions and decisions associated with parenting are defined. We shall also be better placed to decide whether or not parents have a right to send their children to faith schools.

We have already had reason to suppose that the interests of children are not—or at least not necessarily or always—identical to those of their parents. And there are groups, many of whom with strong religious convictions, who regard an education designed to facilitate the development of a child's autonomy as something in which neither they nor their children have any interest whatsoever. Indeed some religious groups see education beyond certain rigidly specifiable limits to be positively anathema. The fact remains, however, that children have a real interest in becoming autonomous. Children are not a mere means to the satisfaction of parental desires. As separate persons, they have an integrity and moral status of their own and it is personal autonomy that provides the rational underpinning for the liberal ideal of respect for persons. To respect someone *as* a person is to respect her right to flourish in the manner of her own choosing. Such a life is impossible where coercion and other constraints on opportunities for choice obtain. If a person's beliefs and values are simply the product of the forces of socialization, or if she simply has no knowledge of other belief systems and ways of life, she cannot possibly be capable of subjecting her beliefs to the level of critical evaluation required of an autonomous person. While it is undeniable that values do not arise *ex nihilo*—we formulate our values, convictions, preferences and objectives as result of exposure, amongst other things, to parents, schools and the media—there is a world of difference between someone whose beliefs and values are accepted merely *because* they are part of the social fabric with which she identifies, and someone who has made those beliefs and values her own as a result of careful reflection on their merits. Those who would frustrate, either intentionally or unwittingly, a child's capacity for independent thought, are denying the child a right to flourish.

Recent philosophy of education is replete with efforts to demonstrate autonomy's instrumental value in helping people lead lives that are worth living. Two such attempts merit particular attention. If we want to live good lives, then according to Eamonn Callan (2002, pp.119ff): 'the capacity to initiate revision of one's conception of the good is necessary if we are to cope with the fallibility of our ethical understanding and the need to adjust our ends to challenging circumstances'. Such a capacity includes the capacity to 'assess ... ethical beliefs and values and, when appropriate, to change belief and conduct accordingly' (Callan, 2002, pp. 119ff).[5] This capacity must, of necessity, reside with the person whose belief system is up for assessment in view of the epistemically privileged perspective that individuals enjoy in determining the extent to which their lives are going well. In other words, it is a requirement of living a good life that one should be able to endorse it for oneself. A good life has to be led not in accordance with other-determined strictures (from the outside) but from the inside.[6]

Brighouse argues for what he calls 'autonomy facilitating education' in order to distinguish it from education designed to *promote* autonomy (2000). He believes that each has a different justificatory strategy. Unlike autonomy facilitating education, autonomy promoting education not only appeals to the civic responsibilities of future citizens but also to the *intrinsic* value of the autonomous life, while the former has a 'character neutrality' aspect. Brighouse admits to having doubts about the coherence and overall sustainability of this distinction especially where the distinction is meant to have practical application, but he is more tenacious in his determination to retain the distinction between the skills and benefits associated with the *opportunity* to live well than those associated with the *habits* of living well. My sympathies are with Callan (2000, p. 126), who believes that the distinction between the instrumental justification of autonomy and its intrinsic value is ultimately unsustainable because: 'people who have learnt to be autonomous find themselves endowed with a character that renders the autonomous self and the end of appropriately asserting autonomy scarcely distinguishable'. For in learning to become autonomous 'we acquire no neutral instrumentality, but a character primed to resist the attractions of heteronomous lives' (Callan, 2000, p. 126).[7]

It would be wrong to infer from the fact of children's incompetence that their parents should have a *carte blanche* to determine the course of their lives. In virtue of their living in such close proximity to their children, parents are, invariably, best placed to know their children and their requirements. Nevertheless there are levels of care to which the child is entitled by reference to which the limitations to be imposed on parental choices should be circumscribed. It would be naive to assume, as does Stephen Gilles, for example, that a parent's knowledge of what is best for her child is necessarily greater than that of the state and its delegates (Gilles, 1996, p. 940). If children's best interests provide one limitation on the extent of parental authority, society's interests in the way children are reared provides another. We therefore require answers to a number of questions before condoning the idea that parents have a right to faith schools. Only a fanatic would systematically set about trying to undermine a child's burgeoning autonomy let alone choose a school with such a warped mission.[8] But there are, as we shall see, noteworthy cases where parents demand such a right. Most parents wanting a faith-based school for their children are no doubt motivated by concerns other than the fanatical, but it would very interesting to know what it is exactly that motivates them in this endeavour. Clearly there is a widespread belief that children in faith schools are better educated in terms of overall results, in spite of the limited evidence in support of this supposition.[9] Many parents also believe that pupils in faith schools are better behaved and more academically motivated than those in secular equivalents. This may or may not be true, but if it is, it should come as no surprise in view of the opportunities for selection available to faith schools. Whatever truth there may be in such matters, in themselves they provide nothing to support the case for parental rights. Another important factor influencing parental choice is the desire to have their children associate with teachers and class mates who share the same *religious* convictions and the opportunities for a specific kind of religious education that such schools afford. And it is *this* that prompts so much concern.

Indoctrination

While this is not the place to embark on a lengthy discussion of such a contested concept as indoctrination, it cannot be denied that faith schools actively foster religious commitment through their assemblies, religious education lessons, and selection of teachers. In the light of avowals by the Church of England to the effect that the Church's mission is 'to bring others into the faith' (Archbishop's Council, 2001, 3.11), that the Church school '*promotes Christian values* through the experience it offers all its pupils' (3.24, italics added), values that will 'run through every area of school life as the writing runs through a stick of rock' (3.25), it is easy to see why the Humanist Philosophers' Group (2001) is concerned about the possible indoctrinatory effects. To account for religious indoctrination in terms of the *intention* to establish belief irrespective of evidence and counter-arguments, as they do, is to presume too much.[10] If children do acquire religious beliefs unquestioningly, out of fear or undue respect of parents and teachers, then they may be said to have been indoctrinated whether or not there was any intention. The key factor is the *likelihood* of children coming to accept the truth of religious propositions given the influences to which they are exposed. Children are not only vulnerable, many are gullible. If, in their formative years, their principal influences are parents and teachers who share the same religious outlook, they are more likely to believe in the truth of religious propositions than they might otherwise have been, and it is unrealistic to suppose that all faith schools would attach priority to ensuring that pupils are encouraged to *critically* reflect on their religious beliefs.[11]

Opinions differ over whether children in faith schools are more likely to be indoctrinated than their peers elsewhere, but it seems to me that the dangers are sufficiently great to cast doubt on whether they should be permitted to operate. Again, it is too easy to slough off the charge with the unwarranted assumption that the products of faith schools are just as capable as other school leavers of subjecting the claims of religion to critical scrutiny. Unfortunately, discussions of autonomy frequently fall short in being confined to cognitive autonomy, the principal concern being with the process by which people come to subscribe to beliefs. Emotional autonomy is no less important when it comes to assessing someone's overall autonomy. It is quite possible, for example, that a one-time Catholic having lost most or all of her faith continues to feel *guilt* about not going to mass or confession. Again, someone who has grown up in a devout Muslim family may well no longer share the convictions of her parents while continuing to *fear* not only their reactions but also placing trust in her own judgements. As Benson (1975, p.14) says: 'intellectual skills cannot exist without qualities of character. The fear and anxiety that subvert the mind in forming judgments also subvert the will in standing by them and translating them into action'. The extent to which parents, teachers and priests exert a powerful influence over children's emotions should not be underestimated. No doubt many faith schools do equip children with the capacity to think for themselves, but restrictions on the capacity for autonomous decision-making exist where there is a mismatch between feelings and beliefs. Similarly, it will not do to suggest that after being subjected to years of faith schooling, children have the right to make up their own minds on religious matters. That is indisputable. But as Susan Moller Okin says: 'individuals must not only be formally free but substantially and more or less equally free to leave their religion or culture of origin; they must have *realistic rights of exit*' (Okin, 2002, p. 206. Cf. Brighouse, 1998, p. 730, italics added).

There are many cultures, not only in Asia and Africa, where girls receive an inferior education to boys, often with religion invoked as justification. Countless numbers of young women are cajoled into marriage with their husband's religion a principal criterion. There are religious groups which openly demand the right to faith schools whereby their children may be socialized (I would say indoctrinated) into adopting specific sex roles with all the associated hierarchies and inequalities and where the right of exit is, in reality, empty rhetoric.

A particularly notorious case of Christian fundamentalist parents who wish to prevent their children from knowing about ways of life other than their own, unless such exposure is accompanied by a statement to the effect that there is only one correct way of life, is that of the Mozert parents in Hawkins County, Tennessee, who, in 1986, obtained the legal right to withdraw their children from reading classes (a right subsequently overturned in the Appeals Court on the grounds that compulsory attendance at such classes violated neither the free exercise nor establishment clauses of the First Amendment). The parents' objections to the reading materials were numerous and included the fact that a boy was seen adopting a role in the kitchen traditionally associated with women, and that they conveyed the message that all human beings had inherent dignity and worth. Above all, they rejected the distinction between exposing their children to ways of life other than their own and the inculcation of a belief in the value of such ways of life. As far as they are concerned, getting children to critically evaluate different ways of life is tantamount to heresy.[12]

A case similar in some respects to that of *Mozert v. Hawkins*, is that of *Wisconsin v. Yoder* in so far as it highlights the problems associated with so-called group rights. A claim not infrequently invoked by cultural minorities is the right to special concessions relating to their children's schooling in order to ensure the continuity of their particular cultural identity. In 1972 the United States Supreme Court ruled in favour of Old Order Amish parents who wanted to withdraw their children from school after the age of 14 on the grounds that attendance after that age would be a violation of their religious freedom and would pose a threat to their way of life. The burden of the Amish case was that exposure to the ways of the world beyond eighth grade 'substantially interferes with the religious development of the Amish child and his integration into the way of life of the Amish faith community' and would undermine the future existence of Amish communities. As to whether this is true or not, the Court's decision[13] not only assumes that children's interests coincide with those of their parents, but also concurs with the view that religious minorities have rights meriting judicial protection. Moreover, the decision makes nonsense of the idea of parent as trustee or, where they fail in their obligations, of the state's responsibilities to children in general. While the Amish clearly satisfy the demands of a liberal society's obligation to accommodate illiberal groups with no desire to impose their values on the rest of us, they should not enjoy a group-right to perpetuate their own existence at the expense of their children's right to the kind of education a liberal democratic society deems appropriate.

Difficulties of defining a 'community' notwithstanding—after all, they are rarely homogenous with clearly defined identities and permanently unchanging ideals— there may be cultural minorities who are perilously close to extinction. And yet it would be fallacious for adult members of such communities to conceive of themselves as *nothing more than* a member of a particular community. In spite of the profound distress felt by someone facing the prospect of her community fizzling out due to the next generation's preference for living in the mainstream culture, there is still no case whatsoever for denying her children their right to a proper education if such a denial were to result in their being prevented from evaluating the pros and cons of living in ways radically at odds with her own. It is all very well, as Piet van der Ploeg reminds us, to speak of–

> the cultural tradition into which one was born (but) it does not follow that people are born *as* members of a cultural community. They are born *in the midst of* members and their culture. (Whether they become) members of a *particular* cultural community is therefore partly the result of education. (van der Ploeg, 1998, p. 181)

In response to the appeal of a religious minority to opt out of state education in accordance with the principle of tolerance, Peter Hobson and John Edwards refer to the–

> logical inconsistency of justifying action that would deny individual freedom of religious choice to their members by employing a principle which upholds that very same freedom, which demonstrates the futility of non-liberal minorities appealing to liberal principles in their demand to have one faith promulgated in their schools. (Hobson and Edwards, 1999, p. 118)

Defenders of faith schools are not lacking in support from philosophers.[14] Both Terence McLaughlin and Mark Halstead share the belief in the importance of children being introduced to what McLaughlin calls an initial 'primary culture' (whereby children receive a 'determinate starting point from conditions of stability as well as openness' towards achieving autonomy, (McLaughlin, 1994, p. 103), which, by extension, entitles them to 'a determinate form of schooling, harmonious with the values and beliefs of the family' (McLaughlin, 1994, p. 106; see also McLaughlin, 1992a, b). As sensitive as he undoubtedly is to a child's need to develop autonomously, McLaughlin is altogether too sanguine about the limited extent to which religious communities might succeed in frustrating this laudable goal (McLaughlin, 2003), or how 'autonomy via faith' can be secured (McLaughlin, 1984). It is all very well to oppose the fixation of beliefs in a child, whereby she is incapable of submitting her beliefs to subsequent criticism, but given the extent to which some people lack emotional autonomy it is easier said than done to ensure that they are capable of 'exit' from their primary culture. Hobson and Edwards are equally sanguine in the confidence they attach to children's ability to critically evaluate alternative religious beliefs given their need for a primary culture. It is too easy to say that parents have a right to 'pass on' their own religious beliefs without knowing more about what this amounts to. There are various ways of passing things on to one's children, not all of which are morally acceptable. What does it mean to encourage children 'to hold their beliefs in an open and flexible way'? (Hobson and Edwards, 1999, p. 114). It is simply unrealistic to believe that parents, while initiating children into their primary (religious) culture, are likely to say things like: 'We'd like you to share our beliefs but only on a *pro tem* basis. Do remain open to what others have to say and be willing to follow the argument wherever it may lead'.

Halstead tries to find a compromise solution to the demand of religious minorities for faith schools as part of the preservation of their cultural identity on the one hand, and on the other, the fears of those who believe that in granting such concessions they would be compromising their principles relating to an education requiring children to be taught the importance of rational debate, the ability to grapple with conflicting world views and to value diversity of tastes which of necessity requires the ability to distance themselves from their primary culture in the interests of autonomous decision-making. Such a compromise would, he believes, require the curriculum to include the following: (i) 'education for democratic citizenship', requiring the recognition of all citizens to fundamental rights and freedoms, as well as the collective duty to support and uphold institutions that embody a shared conception of justice and the rule of law; (ii) 'education for specific cultural attachment', (a) on Rawlsian grounds that citizens may have affections, devotions and loyalties from which they should not distance themselves, (b) because of the presumption of the equal worth of different cultures, and (c) the belief that children, at least in their formative years, need a secure and stable environment where the cultural values of the school are broadly in line with those of the home; (iii) 'education for cross-cultural understanding', designed to provide 'tolerance and respect and the ability to live alongside groups with different cultural values' (Halstead, 1995, pp. 269ff). While (i) and (iii) would be common to both faith and non-faith schools, (ii) would vary from school to school. Clearly (ii) is the most problematic. Not only does Halstead fail to specify the *content* required for such an education, he is the first to concede that there are profound implications for social cohesion. Again, it is far from clear that an education for specific cultural attachment is compatible with (i) and (iii). As Neil Burtonwood succinctly observes: 'These latter two elements are properly concerned with the educational imperative to go beyond culture and this stands in marked contrast to the transisionist concerns of a curriculum for cultural attachment' (Burtonwood, 1996, p. 298).

Halstead is quite right to pose the question 'would any cultural group be barred from establishing schools of their own?' This is a particularly important question as far as government policy in relation to faith schools is concerned. Unless any and every faith is to be subsidized, we need criteria by reference to which particular faiths should be denied public funding. If Christians, Muslims, Jews, Sikhs and the like merit subsidies why not Pagans, especially if their values are not incompatible with those required for democratic citizenship?[15] Halstead is complacent in supposing that 'rivalry and divisiveness would be less likely to thrive in a state which showed equality of respect towards diverse cultural groups and (that) suspicion and resentment between groups would be further diminished by education for cross-cultural understanding' (Halstead, p. 270).

One has only to look at the recent history of Northern Ireland, where most children have so little opportunity to relate to their peers from different religious backgrounds during their formative years, to appreciate how difficult it is to achieve the cross-cultural understanding favoured by Halstead. If faith schools were allowed to proliferate, is it not counter-intuitive to expect that they would be overly concerned with the socially divisive consequences that are more than likely to ensue? Our fears in this respect would be no less misplaced were we to rely on a curriculum that merely teaches *about* other cultures and religions, with actual contact with children from different religious backgrounds having no bearing on the matter. Burtonwood cites the extraordinary comments made by the governors of the Torah Maczikei Hadass School in London who, when criticized by the inspectors for failing to prepare their pupils for the wider society 'simply declared no interest in this particular educational purpose' (Burtonwood, 2003). If we are serious about cross-cultural understanding, why go to the trouble of insulating children from one another during their school years?

It is too easy, in the interests of 'tolerance', to ignore the irrational pressures on young people to conform—not only to the demands of a cultural or religious tradition, but also to those associated with the clamouring materialism of mainstream culture. Such pressures serve to remind us of the state's all-important role in ensuring that future citizens of a democracy acquire the knowledge, skills and capacities required for active citizenship. The implications for public policy, as well as for teachers and parents, are enormous. It is beyond the confines of this chapter to enter the debate concerning the scope and content of civic education, but a democratic state must ensure that children receive an appropriate version as a bulwark against those who, however unwittingly, would deprive young people of opportunities for autonomous well-being. More is required of a system of schooling than the provision of information; strength of will, determination and courage are equally important.[16] Suffice it to say that we have reason to be sceptical about the capacity, and indeed the willingness, of faith schools in this enterprise.

Notes

1. John White cites evidence to suggest that in 1998 only 21% of British people express a belief in God's existence (see HMSO, *Social Trends* 30, in White, 2004, p. 151).

2. Montague relies on a distinction between 'interest' and 'choice' conceptions of rights developed by Sumner (1987). The interest conception depicts parents as beneficiaries of a network of protective and supportive duties shared by others. The genuine interest parents have in protecting the welfare of their children is worth protecting because their children's welfare is worth protecting. The choice conception of rights, on the other hand, would grant parents the right to make decisions concerning their children's well-being only if there is a corresponding area of activity within which parents have moral discretion whether to act. Parents may have the right against society that they not be prevented from fulfilling their obligations towards their children, but this does not extend to denying the right of society to step in when parents fail to fulfil their obligations (cf. Brighouse, 2000, p. 85): 'The right to be allowed to fulfil obligations is precisely that. It does not imply the right to refrain from fulfilling that obligation, nor the right to prevent others from fulfilling their obligations to the same persons.'

3. See, for example, McLaughlin (1994) and Noggle (2002).

4. Autonomous agency is something children acquire over a period and at different stages in their lives. David Archard (1993) provides an excellent account of this. See also Wellman (1997).

5. As Joseph Raz says: '(Autonomy) is an ideal particularly suited to the conditions of the industrial age and its aftermath with their fast changing technologies and free movement of labour … for those of us who live in an autonomy-supporting environment there is no choice but to be autonomous; there is no other way to prosper in such a society' (Raz, 1986, p. 391).

6. As Will Kymlicka puts it: 'paternalistic restrictions on liberty often simply do not work—lives do not go better by being led from the outside, in accordance with values the person does not endorse' (Kymlicka, 1995, p. 81). In similar vein, Raz goes to great lengths to demonstrate the importance for autonomy of participating in the authorship of one's life.

7. Cf. Reich (2002, p. 457, n. 4): '(Brighouse's distinction) strikes me as a classic case of a distinction without a difference. Even accepting Brighouse's claim that autonomy is character neutral and just a set of skills, a notion of autonomy that I find impossible, it is still difficult to see how the teaching of a set of skills that will necessarily be deployed if the state is to be legitimate can be separated from actually promoting the use of the skills'. In a different context, Amy Gutmann argues that a civic education designed with the intention of merely teaching the virtues and skills necessary to deliberate about only *political* issues but not other domains of life, is hopelessly inadequate 'most (if not all) of the same skills and virtues are necessary and sufficient for educating children for citizenship in a liberal democracy are those that are also necessary and sufficient for educating children to deliberate about their way of life' (Gutmann, 1995, p. 573).

8. Fanaticism in an educational context is admirably addressed in Blacker (1998).

9. Citing the research by John Marks (see Marks, 2000), Robert Jackson points out that attainment in literacy and numeracy 'shows the complexity and ambiguity of evidence for higher attainment in Church Schools over against Community Schools', Marks reports that while there is a slightly better average performance in Church Schools than Community Schools, 'there is a huge variation in standards between faith based schools' (Jackson, 2003) (see also Schagen *et al.* (2002).

10. Indoctrination is similarly explicated by Ivan Snook (1972) and John White (1967).

11. The Humanist Philosophers' Group presents a very powerful case against faith schools but relies on an account of 'religious education' as nothing more than 'teaching *about* religion' (2001, p.14, their italics). I have elsewhere argued that in order to be religiously *educated* as opposed to being merely informed or instructed, one needs to *understand* religious concepts such as 'God', 'worship', 'salvation' and so on which itself entails that one is to some extent—the extent depending on the depth of understanding—on the 'inside' of a religion. How could

one understand such concepts in anything other than a superficial sense if one had not been initiated into their possible *use*? I would argue that to understand anything at all about the nature of God is to believe that there is something that counts *as* 'God'—which is another way of saying that understanding presupposes belief. If true, and if it is not the business of a publicly funded system of schooling to get children to believe in the truth of propositions that are highly disputable, then it is difficult to see how there could be a legitimate place for a religious 'education' of this kind. Indeed it is difficult to see how it could be distinguished from indoctrination (Marples, 1978).

12. The Mozerts' claim to have their religious convictions take precedence over an appropriate civic education is vigorously attacked in many places. Stephen Macedo argues that 'children cannot be good citizens of a diverse liberal polity unless they are taught that critical thinking and public argument ... are appropriate means of political justification. Children must ... be exposed to the religious diversity that constitutes our polity for the sake of learning to respect as fellow citizens those who differ from them in matters of religion' (Macedo, 1995a, p. 226). Macedo believes, correctly in my view, that 'a liberal order does not and should not guarantee a level playing field for all the religions and ways of life that people might adopt ... We have no reason to be equally fair to those prepared to accept, and those who refuse to accept, the political authority of public reasons that fellow citizens share' (1995a, p. 227); (a view he defends at greater length in Macedo, 1995b). Similar arguments are deployed with considerable force by Arneson and Shapiro (1996). According to Gutmann (1995, p. 572), a well considered democracy, 'expects us to exercise critical judgment in our willingness to take unpopular political positions, respect reasonable points of view that we reject, and respect public policies from which we dissent. A civic education that satisfies the *Mozert* parents' objections ... would interfere with teaching the virtues and skills of liberal democratic citizenship (such as the teaching of toleration, mutual respect, racial and sexual non-discrimination, and deliberation)' (Gutmann, 1995).

13. A majority verdict with one judge protesting that 'it is the future of the student, not of the parents, that is imperilled by today's decision ... It is the student's judgment, not his parent's, that is essential if we are to give full meaning to ... the right of students to be masters of their own destiny'.

14. Two interesting, but ultimately unsuccessful, attempts to defend the educational rights of religious parents are made by Shelley Burtt (1996) and William Galston (1991)—the latter by reference to liberalism's commitment to toleration and diversity.

15. The *Times Educational Supplement* recently published a letter claiming that Paganism 'is recognised as a religion by the NHS and the Prison Service, both of whom employ Pagan chaplains' (7 November 2003).

16. For an account of what this might involve see Patricia White (1988).

Notes on contributor

Roger Marples is Principal Lecturer in Education and Convener of the Undergraduate Education programme at Roehampton University, UK.

References

Archard, D. (1993) *Children, rights and childhood* (London, Routledge).

Archard, D. (2002) Children, multiculturalism and education, in: D. Archard & C. M MacLeod (Eds) *The moral and political status of children* (Oxford, Oxford University Press).

Archbishops' Council (2001) *The way ahead: Church of England schools in the new millennium* (London, Church House Publishing).

Arneson, R. J. & Shapiro, I. (1996) Democratic autonomy and religious freedom: a critique of *Wisconsin V. Yoder*, in: I. Shapiro & R. Hardin (Eds) *Political order* (New York, New York University Press).

Benson, J. (1975) Who is the autonomous man?, *Philosophy*, 58, 5–17.

Blacker, D. (1998) Fanaticism and education, *American Journal of Education*, 106, 241–271.

Brighouse, H. (1998) Civic education and liberal legitimacy, *Ethics*, 108, 719–745.

Brighouse, H. (2000) *School choice and social justice* (Oxford, Oxford University Press).

Brighouse, H. (2002) What rights (if any) do children have?, in: D. Archard & C. M. MacLeod (Eds) *The moral and political status of children* (Oxford, Oxford University Press).

Burtonwood, N. (2000) Must liberal support for separate schools be subject to a condition of individual autonomy?, *British Journal of Educational Studies*, 48(3), 269–264.

Burtonwood, N. (2003) Social cohesion, autonomy and the liberal defence of faith schools, *Journal of Philosophy of Education*, 37(3), 415–425.

Burtt, S. (1996) In defense of Yoder: parental authority and the public schools, in: I. Shapiro & R. Hardin (Eds) *Political order* (New York, New York University Press).

Callan, E. (2002) Autonomy, child-rearing and good lives, in: D. Archard & C. M. MacLeod (Eds) *The moral and political status of children* (Oxford, Oxford University Press).

DfEE (2001) *Schools: building on success* (Norwich, The Stationery Office, DfES Publications).

Feinberg, J. (1980) The child's right to an open future, in: W. Aiken & H. LaFollette (Eds) *Whose child? Children's rights, parental authority, and state power* (Totowa, NJ, Littlefield, Adams & Co.).

Fried, C. (1878) *Right and Wrong* (Cambridge, MA, Harvard University Press).

Galston, W. (1991) *Liberal purposes: goods, virtue and diversity in the liberal state* (Cambridge, Cambridge University Press).

Gilles, S. (1996) On educating children: a parentalist manifesto, *University of Chicago Law Review*, 63(3), 937–1034.

Griffin, J. (2002) Do children have rights?, in: D. Archard & C. M. MacLeod (Eds) *The moral and political status of children* (Oxford, Oxford University Press).

Gutmann, A. (1995) Civic education and social diversity, *Ethics*, 105, 557–579.

Halstead, M. (1995) Voluntary apartheid? Problems of schooling for religious and other minorities in democratic societies, *Journal of Philosophy of Education* 29(2), 257–272.

Hobson, P. R. & Edwards, J. S. (Eds) (1999) *Religious education in a pluralist society: the key philosophical issues* (London, Woburn Press).

Humanist Philosophers' Group (2001) *Religious schools: the case against* (London, British Humanist Association).

Jackson, R. (2003) Should the state fund faith based schools? A review of the arguments, *British Journal of Religious Education*, 25(2), 89–102.

Kymlicka, W. (1995) *Multicultural citizenship* (Oxford, Oxford University Press).

Macedo, S. (1995a) Multiculturalism for the Religious Right? Defending liberal civic education, *Journal of Philosophy of Education*, 29(2), 223–238.

Macedo, S. (1995b) Liberal civic education and religious fundamentalism: the case of God v. John Rawls?, *Ethics* 105, 468–496.

Marks, J. (2001) Standards in Church of England, Roman Catholic and LEA schools in England, in: J. Burn, J. Marks, P. Pilkington & P. Thompson (Eds) *Faith in education* (London, Civitas).

Marples, R. (1978) Is religious education possible?, *Journal of Philosophy of Education*, 12, 81–91.

McLaughlin, T. (1984) Parental rights and the upbringing of children, *Journal of Philosophy of Education*, 18(1), 75–83.

McLaughlin, T. (1992a) The ethics of separate schools, in: M. Leicester & M. J. Taylor (Eds) *Ethics, ethnicity and education* (London, Kogan Page).

McLaughlin, T. (1992b) The distinctiveness of Catholic education, in: T. McLaughlin, J. M. O'Keefe & B. O'Keefe (Eds) *The contemporary Catholic school: context, identity and diversity* (London, Falmer Press).

McLaughlin, T. (1994) The scope of parents'6 educational rights, in: M. Halstead (Ed.) *Parental choice and education: principles, policy and practice* (London, Kogan Page).

McLaughlin, T. (2003) An extra-liberal(?) stance to philosophy of education: adding to, or going beyond, liberalism?, *Journal of Philosophy of Education,* 37(1), 174–180.

Montague, P. (2000) The myth of parental rights, *Social Theory and Practice,* 26(1), 47–68.

Noggle, R. (2002) Special agents: children's autonomy and parental authority in: D. Archard & C. M. MacLeod (Eds) *The moral and political status of children* (Oxford, Oxford University Press).

Nozick, R (1989) *The examined life: philosophical meditations* (New York, Simon & Schuster).

Okin, S. M. (2002) 'Mistresses of their own destiny': group rights, gender, and realistic rights of exit, *Ethics,* 112, 205–230.

Raz, J. (1986) *The morality of freedom* (Oxford, Oxford University Press).

Reich, R. (2002) Opting out of education: Yoder, Mozert, and the autonomy of children, *Educational Theory,* 52(4), 445–461.

Schagen, S., Davies, D., Rudd, P. & Schagen, I. (2002) *The impact of specialist and faith schools on performance* (Slough, National Foundation for Educational Research).

Schoeman, F. (1980) Rights of children, rights of parents, and the moral basis of the family, *Ethics,* 91, 6–19.

Snook, I. (1972) *Indoctrination and education* (London, Routledge & Kegan Paul).

Sumner, L. W. (1987) *The moral foundation of rights* (Oxford, Clarendon Press).

Van der Ploeg, P. (1998) Minority rights and educational authority, *Journal of Philosophy of Education,* 32(2), 177–193.

Wellman, C. (1997) *An approach to rights* (Dordrecht, Kluwer).

White, J. (1967) Indoctrination, in: R. S. Peters (Ed.) *The concept of education* (London, Routledge & Kegan Paul).

White, J. (2004) Should religious education be a compulsory school subject?, *British Journal of Religious Education,* 26(2), 151–164.

White, P. (1988) Educating courageous citizens, *Journal of Philosophy of Education,* 22(1), 67–74.

PART B: SYMPOSIUM: USING REFLECTION TO FIND ONESELF AND THE BIG PICTURE

COMMENTARY (2)

Reflecting and talking about private lives and professional consequences

Helen Johnson

Mature individuals would claim that they are continuously and continually engaged in a process of reflective practice. All of us think about what has happened today to reach some conclusion about how that experience should affect or influence what we do and how we do it in the future. However, its advocates would claim that reflexivity as a conscious reflective practice is more than that informal consideration of how we have dealt with today's events or crises or happenings. Reflective practice is the integration of thought and action with reflection (Imel, 1989). Such integration causes there to be something going on that is rigorous and demanding. Evaluation and decision-making is to be informed, logical and systematic. According to Taggart and Wilson (1998, p. 2) reflective thinking can be grouped:

> according to the mode of thinking or the process an individual progresses through to reach a level of reflection that complements both the context of the situation and the background the individual brings to the episode.

While there is a debate about whether a hierarchy of thinking exists, and if so, the exact delineation of that stratification, there is a general agreement (Taggart and Wilson, 1998) 'on three modes or levels of reflective thinking: technical, contextual and dialectical'. Van Manen (1977) talks of a *technical* rationality that seeks precedence and information from past experiences that concentrates on the actuality of behaviour, content and skill. Essentially, the technical is *doing*. He goes on to see the second level of reflection in terms of the *context*. In a sense, the relatively unproblematic nature of the technical gives way to the problems and issues arising from belief and value systems of the practitioner or protagonist. Here, as Taggart and Wilson (1998) point out, there is a necessity to make comparisons and choices, and in this, decision-making will be based on knowledge and value commitments, in which professional (and perhaps, personal) principles are validated. Van Manen's (1977) third level of reflectivity critically addresses issues at a *dialectical* level, in which ethical or sociopolitical or moral issues are confronted and examined. At this level, according to Taggart and Wilson (1998, p. 5), practitioners consider issues of this kind, but any *personal bias* is eliminated as: 'the ability to make defensible choices and view an event with open-mindedness is also indicative of reflecting at a dialectical level'.

One of the most influential writers in this area is Donald Schon (1983, 1988), who has drawn on 'an historical foundation in a tradition of learning supported by Dewey, Lewin and Piaget' (Imel, 1989). With these origins, it is evident that reflective practice and its thinking is constructivist. In this, as Brooks and Brooks (1993, quoted in Taggart and Wilson, 1998, p. 9), would say:

> ...all knowledge is constructed and invented by the learner; involves all learners in active manipulations of meanings, numbers and patterns; believes learning is non-linear; provides students with tools of empowerment: concepts, heuristic procedures, self-motivation and reflection; and believes learning occurs most effectively through guided discovery, meaningful application, and problem solving.

In many small research projects, the sole researcher is usually left very much alone (though not without access to the support of 'critical friends') when designing and completing the task. If the research project would seem to sit totally under a constructivist umbrella, it is also evident that Knowles' work (1990) on a theory of adult learning—an andragogy—shares the same ground. But additionally, in his view, the adult learner, in whatever guise, has to *need* to know. All learning engaged in by adults will be assessed in terms of its 'benefits, consequences, and risks'. This assessment will undertaken *before* 'involvement in the learning situation'. Knowles stressed that it was the 'self-concept and intellectual responsibility' of adults as learners that supported and was entirely appropriate for 'self-directed learning situations'. Knowles goes on to emphasise that experiential learning based on 'the adult learner's *past* experiences is essential' (p. 34). However, at its widest level, in the lay view mentioned by Phillips and Pugh (2000, p. 41), research is 'finding out something you don't know'. But how can something new and unknown be found if the starting point of this learning is things experienced in the past? It is here that Schon's (1988) ideas about reflective practice can come fully into play.

According to Schon, there are two types of reflection. Firstly, there is reflection on action, in which the practitioner reflects *following* action or in an interruption; and secondly, there is reflection in action that is engaged in *during* the event or situation. (In a similar vein, Kottkamp (1990) uses the terms 'offline' and 'online'). Both forms of reflection would seem to be a process entirely appropriate for the qualitative process. But, looking more closely, what of reflection on action: how long in the past should be the experiences under consideration and can they be drawn from the hinterland far beyond the immediate core of current and immediate action? Here lie issues of consideration, reflection and discarding.

On a personal level, certainly, we have all spent much time reflecting ('off-line and 'on-line') on issues that were directly relevant and on those that, at best, were tangential. However, though the process would have been much more focused and so completed more quickly, we can say that we have benefited from a 'free-form' reflection that has not used technical, contextual and dialectical thinking in any sequential way. Follow-up investigations and reading—that have linked seeming incongruities— have, on occasion, taken us out of our immediate field. Of course, it is time-consuming, confusing and misleading. Such reflection can result in a seeming lack of focus within an academic exercise. But it can also develop into a process that led us as adult learners and as researchers through a body of knowledge that has become distilled into a professional and personal philosophy, that is derived from a wide view of life experience. Though difficult to manage because of the range and depth of the available sources, this can only enrich the process.

So, for the adult learner/researcher engaged in reflection a meaningful question is to ask why *this* area of experience has been chosen rather than *that*. There are going to be many answers, many of which are likely to be logical, rational and pragmatic. We, as adult learners and researchers, could also be revisiting, within the reflection process, some issues that we may have experienced in a situation similar to the context in which *this* reflection is set. Or, perhaps more interestingly in terms of personal development, we could be revisiting a set of issues that *first* arose in a *context that is entirely dissimilar* to that being currently experienced.

Given these considerations, how is this reflection to be managed and resolved? On a general level, Roth (1989) has offered several strategies for reflective practice. Not surprisingly, he recommends *questioning*. So, here is another context, in which we are to go beyond the 'taken for grantedness' of 'everyday life' that Berger and Berger (1972) have explained in their discussion of the sociology of Alfred Schutz. These questions are to ask about the *what* and *why* of events and situations. In the answers, alternatives are to be compared and contrasted—and in all this, the underlying theoretical framework and rationale are to be sought.

Posner (1996, p. 10) states that: 'more learning is derived from reflecting on an experience than is derived from the experience itself'. Specific tools can be used in this reflective practice. Writing it down in the form of, say, reflective journalling helps turn reflection into a more coherent and revisitable educational experience. Another tool that is similar is reflection in the form of life histories or autobiographical sketches (Olson, 1988). They are a narrative strategy that practitioners can use to explore 'the background the individual brings to the episode' (Taggart and Wilson, 1998, p. 2) and their own received wisdom or self-developed theories about learning. Importantly, Taggart and Wilson (1998, p. 164) state that:

> The perspective of education brought out in the practitioner's story line is based on beliefs, intentions, interpretations, and *interactions of a lifetime*. An autobiographical frame of reference assists practitioners in making sense of current experiences and responding rationally to stimuli within those experiences. (My italics)

Many additional advantages can be claimed for autobiographical narrative or life history as a device to prompt and encourage reflection and learning. Significantly given the folios of this book, Taggart and Wilson (1998, p. 164) assert, on a general level, that the writing of narratives can offer: 'reclamation, emancipation and empowerment … self-understanding, personal growth and professional development'. More specifically, they argue that such a device can specifically also enhance 'qualitative research by opening new avenues of thought'.

The reflective journal and autobiographical narratives, as developmental devices, can be expressed in any manner that is useful to the adult learner and researcher. How should they be expressed *here*? Are they clearly separate, in a different more personal and relaxed tone to the formality of the academic mainstream? Or can they be incorporated? Phillips and Pugh (2000, p. 59) remind us of Olson's remark that writing is 'the means of discovery of new knowledge'. Richardson (1994, p. 516) takes up this point:

> I consider writing as a method of inquiry, a way of finding out about yourself and your topic. Although, we usually think about writing as a mode of 'telling' about the social world, writing up is not just a mopping-up activity at the end of the research project. Writing is also a way of 'knowing'—a method of discovery and analysis. By writing in different ways, we discover new aspects of our topic and our relationship to it. Form and content are inseparable.

Phillips and Pugh (2000, p. 59) temper this view by reminding us of typical remarks of academics that 'good writing can't cure bad thought'. However, they go on to note that:

> Several eminent psychologists interviewed by Cohen (1977) said that the only time they think is when they write and Murray (1978) reports that this is also true of poets and authors. He suggests it may be true of all writing.

Qualitative research allows more personal, individual and subjective data to be collected. Denzin (1994) sees qualitative research as a set of interpretative practices with a naturalistic approach. According to Richardson (1994, p. 516), qualitative research is nothing unless it is fluid: 'The present moment is defined by a new sensibility, the core of which doubts that any discourse has a privileged place, any method or theory a universal and general claim to authoritative knowledge'. This is an approach that stresses an unrepentant pragmatism instead of a self-conscious rigour. It takes a wide, strategic view while placing an emphasis on the self-reflexive; because of this, qualitative research is 'inherently multi-method'. Brewer and Hunter (1989, p. 25) list the methods open to the qualitative researcher. They include personal experience, introspection, interview, autobiographical narratives/ life history—and reflective practice. So, we turn now to examples of such reflections that have relevance to faith schools and other educational institutions. Four professionals will explore the links between their private selves and their professional activities, as they strive to understand what they do for children and young people in a variety of educational institutions and wider contexts—from a declared ethical, moral and religious basis. In pursuit of one individual truth about the impact of being a student at a faith school, an interview with a former faith school student, who is preparing to join the teaching profession himself, asks some very direct questions and gets some equally direct answers.

Notes on contributor

Helen Johnson is Reader in Education, School of Education, Kingston University, UK.

References

Berger, P. & Berger, B. (1976) *Sociology: a biographical approach* (Harmondsworth, Penguin).

Brewer, J. & Hunter, A. (1989) *Multimethod research: a synthesis of styles* (Newbury Park, CA, Sage).

Brooks, J. & Brooks, M. (1993) *In search of understanding: the case for constructivist classrooms* (Alexandria, VA, Association for Supervision and Curriculum Development).

Cohen, D. (1977) *Psychologists on psychology* (London, Routledge & Kegan Paul).

Denzin, N. (1994) The art and politics of interpretation, in: N. Denzin & Y. Lincoln (Eds) *Handbook of qualitative research* (London, Sage).

Imel, S. (1989) Teaching adults: is it different? ERIC Digest No. 82, Columbus, USA ERIC Clearinghouse on Adult, Career and Vocational Education (ED 305 495).

Knowles, M. (1990) *The adult learner: a neglected species* (4th edn) (Houston, TX, Gulf).

Kottkamp, R. (1990) Means for reflection, *Education and Urban Society*, 22(2), 82–203.

Murray, D. (1978) Internal revision: a process of discovery, in: C. Cooper & L. Oddell (Eds) *Research on composing* (Urbana, IL, NCTE).

Olson, J. (1988) Making sense of teaching: cognition vs. culture, *Journal of Curriculum Studies*, 12, 1–11.

Phillips, E. & Pugh, D. (2000) *How to get a PhD* (3rd edn) (Buckingham, Open University Press).

Posner, G. (1996) *Field experience: a guide to reflective teaching* (White Plains, NY, Longman).

Richardson, L. (1994) Writing: a method of inquiry, in: N. Denzin & Y. Lincoln (Eds) *Handbook of qualitative research* (London, Sage).

Roth, R. (1989) Preparing the reflective practitioner: transforming the apprentice through the dialectic, *Journal of Teacher Education*, 40(2), 31–35.

Schon, D. (1983) *The reflective practitioner* (New York, Basic Books).

Schon, D. (1988) *Educating the reflective practitioner: toward a new design for teaching and learning in the professions* (San Francisco, CA, Jossey-Bass).

Taggart, G. & Wilson, A. (1998) *Promoting reflective thinking in teaching* (Thousand Oaks, CA, Corwin Press Inc.).

Van Manen, M. (1977) Linking ways of knowing with ways of being practical, *Curriculum Inquiry,* 6(3), 205–228.

Moral imperatives, professional interventions and resilience, and educational action in chaotic situations: the souls of children amidst the horror of war

Catherine M. Hill

Every now and then I ask myself to what degree Sayonara's spirit and sensibility weren't blinded by her crushing past. How could she cry for her brother without bleeding to death? How could she love without kindling horror? There are insights that can destroy you, and the worst death is rarely your own. In this country marked by violence, we have learned that one of two things can happen to a child who witnesses the atrocious death of family members: either he is carbonized or he becomes illuminated. If he is carbonized he is reduced to half a person, but if he is illuminated he can become a person and a half. (Restrepo, 1999, p. 209)

Shaping lives through situation and context

Common sense tells us that cognitive and spiritual lives do not develop in a vacuum, isolated from environmental influences. Thus, few children have the possibility of an open future. For the heaviest hand of all influences that beats upon our children is the harsh and cruel hand of war. When the Vietnam War was part of the nightly newscast of my own adolescence, there was an oft-repeated popular slogan, 'war is not healthy for children and other living things'. Certainly there is no argument against that. Gross violations against children continue unabated. Murder, rape, HIV/AIDS, mutilation, forced recruitment, displacement, terror, the proliferation of small arms, landmines and light weapons, personal injury and malnourishment are just some of the most visible examples (Machel, 2001, pp. 3–15). Likewise, in our purportedly civilized homelands, it is painfully clear that children harbor anxieties, fears, worries, ideas, facts and figures from what they hear, see and sense in the unsettling world around them (Coloroso, 2003).

In recent decades I have witnessed forms of armed conflict (Armstrong, 2002) inevitably affecting children in places like Bogota and Beirut (Al-Shaykh, 1995) and Bosnia (Blackman, 1997). What has occurred, and in some places continues, cannot be studied or discussed with quick summaries or easy judgments and remedies. We have a moral imperative to reflect what we have seen first-hand (or through the media), acknowledge our collective responsibility to rescue, recover and protect the children, and to act with urgency.

Psychologically and physically, children are maimed and exploited more brutally and systematically than ever before (Hastie, 1997). They get caught up in and criminalized by complex conflicts and endemic struggles for power and resources with no distinction made for combatant or civilian. The so-called 'collateral damage' of modern warfare suffered by civilians in general and children in particular (Moses *et al.*, 2003) has risen from approximately 5% in the 1940s to 90% in the 1990s (United Nations Children Data Management). Conservative contemporary estimates provided by the United Nations reveal that over 20 million children worldwide are currently uprooted from their homes or internally displaced. Millions more are disabled, orphaned and given an HIV/AIDS death sentence. Furthermore, over 300,000 are forcibly engaged as child soldiers. What do child soldiers do? The Child Soldiers Research Project (UNICEF) reports that these young fighters are programmed for a cycle of violence. They provide labor, spy and carry messages, guard prisoners, kill and rape, provide sex, and become martyrs. Their return to communities often exacerbates local fears for safety (Barnitz, 1999). How, if at all, can our children be rescued, recovered and cared for so that they not be carbonized but illuminated for whatever remains of their shattered lives? Surely, when children are cared for emotionally, guided ethically, made safe physically, and equipped with the social and vocation al skills needed to negotiate responsible lives in an increasingly complex and perilous world, they are more likely to become good persons and great souls. Still, the question remains: to what extent can children who have been criminalized recover from the devastation of their lives? Violence is as complex and varied as the persons who experience it. Hence, there is no easy answer or formula for those of us who care enough to actively address the social, psychological, political and cognitive needs of children of desperate circumstances. Nonetheless, we—the educational leaders of our time—need to act on behalf of the children. Our collective commitment to and perseverance in policy development, political advocacy, research and field practice will improve standards for the recovery and protection of children (Apfel & Simon, 2002).

You may ask why this topic? Why this focus? In all the years of recorded history, the earthly world has been at peace for a total of twenty nine years (Hedges, 2003) leaving countless souls physically and spiritually emaciated in the wake of war. Chris Hedges has reported watching soldiers entice children 'like mice into a trap and murder them for sport' (Hedges, 2003, p. 94). Over the last four years, chance circumstances brought me to Beirut, Bogota, Belfast, Damascus, villages throughout Jordan, as well as New York and New Jersey after September 11. Throughout this journey I met children, adolescents and young adults—some remarkably survived indignities and atrocities with courage and resilience, while others appeared defeated and daunted. Since then, the ultimate academic question haunts me—*why*? Moving beyond the question, I must ask, what can we do to reclaim the child survivors, to maximize their recovery and resilience so they can learn well, live strong, and have a chance at becoming good persons and great souls. As Emerson (1860) reminds us, a great soul will be strong to live, as well as strong to think. The facilitation of growth toward greatness of mind and spirit is, I repeat, the moral imperative of educational leaders everywhere. The words and wisdom of a Ugandan schoolgirl call to us: 'If I tell you, you cannot feel the pain of this suffering, if you do not see it physically. If you only glance at it, a sword will pierce your heart'.

Focus: witnessing Bogota

While I have talked with children and studied their situations in multiple areas of the world, it is Bogota that I have come to know the best. Civil war in Colombia dates back well over fifty years with the assassination of President-elect Jorge Gaitan in 1948. Violence among liberals, conservatives and communists predates drug trafficking, but it has intensified and spread as multiple factions (the Revolutionary Armed forces of Colombia (FARC), the National Liberation Army (ELN), local paramilitary armies) fight over power and profits. In the words of one human rights activist, 'Colombia is just another one of those places where a lot of bad things happen and there is no cure'. She went on to say that:

> It should matter to anyone who is American, for reasons that are rooted in the way Americans think and live and do business in the world. This is why: Our pleasures are tearing Colombia apart. Our leisure funds terror. Our parties pull Colombia under, as surely as a stone sinks cloth in water. Colombia provides coffee for Starbucks, fresh flowers for homes, emeralds for the rich, but primarily cocaine and heroin for the streets ($46+ billion annually). (Kirk, 2003)

Colombia has narco-mayors, narco-police, narco-malls, narco-hotels, narco-highways, narco-airlines, narco-parks, narco-nuns, narco-beauty pageants, narco-singers, narco-horses, and narco-children, who carry pounds of heroin through airports in the USA (Kirk, 2003). What is happening in Colombia exceeds familiar tales of Latin corruption and savagery.

Caught in the crossfire of this culture of violence are the children—both rich and poor. The children of the rich are kidnapped almost daily by guerrilla groups and held for ransom to fund their terror activities. Some of the children are returned, having been raped, starved and assaulted. Others disappear into the mountainous jungles never to be seen or heard from again. The children of the poor are taken from their families by force and indoctrinated as 'soldiers'—some as young as five years old. To escape the violence of rebel factions, hundreds of thousands of rural villagers and farmers have descended upon Bogota, building shacks on the hills surrounding the city, and living on the garbage collected off the streets (Kirk, 2003).

A moral purpose in trying to make things better

Priests, nuns and humanitarian employees work against time and short resources to palliate the worst of the war's damage. Some, notably Father Frank in Medellin and Sister Tierney in Bogota, operate Catholic schools where they try to meet the children's basic needs for food and clothing while also working to rehabilitate their souls and psyches. Importantly, Father Frank and Sister Tierney have the power of their churches behind them to support their work. This support can be drawn on to restore *their own* resilience in the face of the endless chaos. It has to be noted that the humanitarian workers of Proyecto de Vida have no such foundation of support. Further on, I will tell you of the work they all do and the children they serve with minimal resources and enormous hearts.

Colombian children, like children everywhere, have great cognitive and spiritual potential (Coles, 1997). Their major disadvantage is to have been born amid poverty and violence. One father, a recent refugee to the city, told the story of his plight. He had been working in the fields when the army approached his house where his wife and five daughters were working. Believing that guerillas were inside, the army fired upon the home, killing his 11-year-old daughter and seriously crippling his wife and five-year-old daughter. He related the following:

> I asked the Colonel to please deliver to me the daughters who were not wounded. For six days, he tricked me saying he would bring them, until finally he insulted me and never brought them ... The army finished off my crop, they killed my cattle. And to top it off, my dead daughter's body disappeared, they never gave her back to me.

Here, children and adults are pushed to the limit of what is monstrous and unthinkable. Upon his return to New York after fieldwork in Colombia, the noted anthropologist, Michael Taussig, observed the following:

> This very day I read that in eighteen months under Ariel Sharon's rule, some 1,300 Palestinians and Israelis have been killed. We think of Israel as a bloody siege, and our heart stops in our mouth. Meanwhile, in a small Colombian town of 50,000 people, quietly and unnoticed by the world at large, over 300 people have been assassinated in one year. (Taussig, 2003, p. 188)

Hundreds of thousands of families have attempted to escape the horrors of their country's civil war by taking refuge in the city of Bogota. Some find work, move in with extended families, and send their children to school. The poorest of the poor build temporary shacks of discarded plastic and pieces of wood and metal found along the roadside. Once *supposedly* safe in Bogota, their cruelest enemy becomes relentless despair. The workers of the Fundacion Proyecto de Vida [Life Plan Foundation] know intimately the increasingly grim prospects that the children face due to difficult family, education, social and economic conditions. Hence, they set into motion a plan known as 'the integral protection of children whose rights have been violated'. These are children who do not have the money or the preparation to attend schools: their only hope is the '*proyecto*', now in three locations throughout Bogata—Usaquen, Ciudad Bolivar, and Soacha. Approximately 500 children (ages 4 to 20) participate in project activities designed to promote education in the care of their bodies, self-expression, and the strengthening of mental and physical abilities. The overall stated mission of the project is to protect children who live under particularly difficult and trying circumstances and whose basic human rights have been violated. These children are provided with guidance and the spaces and the means that will promote their integral development through the acquisition of social, cognitive, emotional, physical and transcendental skills that will allow them to build a life plan for themselves (Coles, 1997). Children are led to discover their talents through participation in creative activities such as dance, theatre, music, plastic arts, yoga and relaxation exercises. In a climate of affection, communication and non-conventional learning opportunities, children are led to believe in themselves and reach beyond the misery and despair of their lives (Antonovsky, 1987).

The guiding principles of the project include: (1) focus on the children (without any type of discrimination); (2) excellence (in everything they do); (3) competitive position (always reaching for more); (4) operational style (when necessary, procedures are adapted transparently and honestly to meet the needs of the children); (5) innovation (new and effective strategies are sought ongoing); ethical behavior (daily activities out with the highest of ethical standards); (7) transparency (public evaluation and accountability are invited); and (8) respect (the principles of tolerance, fair treatment, respect for all human beings and diversity of thought permeate the organization and its efforts). Who are the children of *el proyecto*? Meet Oscar, age 12. When he first came to the program, he admits that he did not write, speak or behave well. Now he is in the sixth grade, and with a smile says that he 'want[s] the most to be a good person in order to earn the love of people, and also to be a great soccer player'. Meet Astrid Marisol, age 10: Astrid was invited into the program by a friend six years ago. She wants 'to do big things for others', like: 'working for the poor and for the children in order for them to have good thoughts and to take the straight path and not the wrong path in life'. Astrid has come to believe that when you have dreams, and the will to make them come true, there is nothing that can stop you. She hopes to become a nurse someday. Amidst adversity that seems insurmountable is the making of great souls in the barrios of Bogota.

Focus: witnessing Beirut

Civil war raged in Lebanon from 1975. Over a 15-year period, entire towns were destroyed and thousands of people killed—many of them civilians picked off by snipers of unknown affiliation. Previously existing divisions among religious groups grew deeper as civilians were forced to carry identification cards tying them to a religious group and political affiliation. Prior to 1975, children played with one another, studied side-by-side, and sometimes married 'the Other'. The war, however, brought a painful halt to any mingling of faiths and political persuasions. Post-war Lebanon is filled with stories of complicated friendships, senseless detentions, and encounters marked by violence and kindness. The world watched with indifference or, in some cases, with revulsion, while providing more and more weapons. There, as in all other war-torn places, the women and children have borne the weight of one life-threatening situation after another (Awwad, 1989). The women have had to provide domestic supplies, deal with wrecked homes, create alternative shelters, cope with and explain to those left behind the tragedy of death and destruction. Furthermore, they continued to educate the children in the absence of schools, and do what they can to keep the minds and souls of children alive with some vision of hope. When I first came to Beirut in the summer of 1999, the physical and psychological consequences of war were still visible (Makdisi, 1999). In the people with whom I spent time, remembrances surfaced without warning and were felt without mercy. Palestinian camps, likewise, remained places of unrest and uncertainty. The general amnesty of 1991, along with acts of forgiveness tempered by patient humor, are giving way to acceptance and civility.

Researchers into Lebanon's trauma found children who were exposed to shelling, destruction of home, death and forced displacement were twice as likely to manifest regression, depression and aggressive behaviors than those without such exposure. But the outcome is not destiny. Trauma, as Antonovsky (1987) points out, can produce 'salutogenic' or health-promoting forces, as well as 'pathogenic' or destructive ones. Psychologically informed interventions by caring adults can shift the balance between pathogenic and salutogenic forces by fostering resilience in children. It is the difference between being carbonized or illuminated. Everything has changed in the world and nothing has changed. If the war is no longer here, it is somewhere else. And the child who lives through it becomes the stained and/or strengthened adult who bears raw and undigested memories.

Focus: witnessing Bosnia

In 1991, as federation states of the former Yugoslavia began to declare independence, war erupted with a vengeance, pitting Bosnian Croats, Muslims and Serbs against one another. The years that followed were marked by 'ethnic cleansing', siege, displacement and death. The Bosnian War left a quarter of a million people dead and hundreds of thousands displaced.

Deep-rooted prejudices of the people (Croats against Serb against Muslims and urbanites against rural dwellers) remain major blocks to the integration of displaced peoples and the restoration of schooling and employment. Children, teenagers, single parents, ethnic minorities, elderly people and the mentally ill were neglected by the efforts of aid and governmental agencies (Blackman, 1997). As in Beirut, divisions along religious, social and political lines that were previously insignificant now loomed as causes to kill, destroy and subject 'the Other'. The human stories of the remarkable, valiant and long-suffering Bosnian people are all too familiar. The damaged, confused and disabled children are left behind in the wake of devastation. Bosnian society remains unstable and humanitarian agencies are uncertain as to how they can best approach the suffering people so as to contribute in some way to their healing and restoration. Theories are solid and accessible but reality is the big problem. Long-term development work is the hallmark of the future in Bosnia.

Implications for education

My discussion of the situation in Bogota, in particular, pinpointed the efforts of educationalists running schools and working from an ethical and religious basis. Are there some more general principles to be identified from these three cases (and others)? Considering how best to care for children of conflict—both near and far away—requires educational practitioners and researchers to look at remedies internationally, nationally and locally. The psychosocial recovery programs advocated by the UN agencies, NGOs and others (Brooks & Goldstein, 2001, 2003a, b) are delivered from an ethical and moral basis. They follow guiding principles of this type:

(1) Human rights: All programs for recovery must respect the rights of children according to the Convention on the Rights of the Child (CRC).
(2) Non-discrimination: Programs should be provided to all children without discrimination, particularly insuring the inclusion of girls and especially oppressed, disadvantaged and disabled children.
(3) Best interests of the child: In all decisions and peace-making treaties, primary considerations should be given to the psychological and social well-being of the child, consistent with the CRC.
(4) Values and culture: Programs should be based on a situational assessment that includes information about the culture and values of the community into which the child is being reintegrated.
(5) Child participation: Children need to participate in their own recovery, to join in groups with others, to express opinions and views, and to have access to information and knowledge.
(6) Family and community: Participation of families and communities will contribute to the long-term recovery of children. The value of family and community ownership of the process should not be underestimated.
(7) Long-term commitment and continuity: capacity-building strategies must be incorporated in all phases of programming.
(8) Partnership: Civil societies, agencies and national and local government should work in partnership on behalf of the children.

During the chaos of conflict, education for survival and development as outlined above can create a zone of safety and security for children. It can take the simple shape of organized play or the more complex form of high-order critical thinking. Whether simple or complex, education is a life-affirming activity and it is vitally important that it continue in the midst of conflict. A recent World Bank study found that increases in school enrolment contribute to the safety of the community and reduce the probability of armed conflict. Education can change the world. Financing it is a complex challenge because it requires the will to do so. Schools everywhere have the capacity to undertake the groundwork for creating peaceful societies. They are the places where children learn negotiation, problem-solving, critical thinking and communication and life skills.

Clearly education contributes to trauma healing. Some children who have lived through unspeakable horrors and traumas collapse and fade or, as Restrepo (1999) reminds us, carbonize. It must be noted that, on the other hand, others turn out to be healthy, vibrant, wise and illuminated. There is substantial research literature on the phenomenon of resiliency in children (for example, Brooks & Goldstein, 2003b). The important outcome is the suggestion that it might be possible to foster resiliency, as Apfel and Simon (1996) indicate. What qualities should we foster and what interventions might we employ to do so? They recommend the following:

(1)   Resourcefulness. People who are resourceful can make something out of nothing, using imagination and whatever resources are available. This includes the tangible and intangible; resourceful people are able to locate human warmth and kindness—even in enemies or persecutors.
(2)   Ability to attract and use adult support. Resilient children have significant adult(s) in their lives. These adults assist them in discovering an early sense of power and competence. The interaction experienced by these children and adults is generative.
(3)   Curiosity and intellectual mastery. Knowledge is power and knowing about the crisis that engulfs and threatens a child increases the child's ability to survive. The trade-off is this: choosing to bear the anxiety of pain in looking and finding out for the sake of long-term relief, in place of the short-term remedy afforded by avoidance and denial.
(4)   Compassion—but with detachment. This means, for example, that a child can feel compassion for a parent or caretaker who may well be disturbed or out of control. Detachment refers to the safe distance that such a child intuitively keeps.
(5)   Ability to conceptualize. To conceptualize an atrocity helps to diminish feelings of isolation because the child can see the occurrence as something affecting others as well.
(6)   Conviction of one's right to survive. The sense of *survival merit* gives the child the feeling that he or she was permitted to live for some special purpose.
(7)   Ability to remember and invoke images of good and sustaining figures. The memories of special people, family and community stories can sustain an individual through tragic times.

(8) A goal to live for. This is reminiscent of Victor Frankl's work on man's search for meaning: give me a why, and I will find the how.

(9) The need and ability to help others. The meaning of this key factor echoes the age-old adage that to give is to receive. The pathogenic contrast is what Martin Seligman calls 'learned helplessness' (1998).

(10) An affective repertory. The particular behavior associated with survival is the ability to laugh and not cry until a safer time. Interventions must first help a child to survive. Then what we want for them is to experience some measure of well-being in knowing they are loved and cared for. Once that happens, a child can thrive regardless of what he or she has witnessed or lived through. However, none of the aforementioned bits and pieces of hope can be held and cherished in a child's life, mind and spirit, without the mediation, inspiration and intervention of a significant and caring adult.

> The lives of all of us are stories.
> If enough of these stories are told,
> Then perhaps we will begin to see
> That our lives are the same story.
> The differences are merely in the details. (Julius Lester, in Armstrong, 2002, p. 52)

Notes on contributor

Catherine Hill is Associate Dean of Liberal Arts and Science and Associate Professor of Educational Leadership at Villanova University, Villanova, Pennsylvania, USA.

References

Al-Shaykh, H. (1995) *Beirut blues* (New York, Doubleday).

Antonovsky, A. (1987) *Unraveling the mystery of health: how people manage stress and stay well* (San Francisco, CA, Jossey-Bass Publishers).

Apfel, R. & Simon, B. (Eds) (1996) *Minefields in their hearts: the mental health of children in war* (New Haven, CT, Yale University Press).

Armstrong, B. (Ed.) (2002) *Shattered: stories of children and war* (New York, Alfred A. Knopf).

Awwad, T. Y. (1989) *Death in Beirut* (Washington DC, Three Continents Press).

Barnitz, L. A. (1999) *Child soldiers: youth who participate in armed conflict* (Washington DC, Youth Advocate Program International).

Blackman, E. (1997) *Harvest in the snow: my crusade to rescue the lost children of Bosnia* (Dulles, VA, Brassey's Inc.).

Brooks, R. & Goldstein, S. (2001) *Raising resilient children* (New York, Contemporary Books).

Brooks, R. & Goldstein, S. (2003a) *The power of resilience* (New York, McGraw-Hill).

Brooks, R. & Goldstein, S. (2003b) *Nurturing resilience in our children* (New York, Contemporary Books).

Coles, R. (1997) *The moral intelligence of children* (New York, Random House).

Coloroso, B. (2003) *The bully, the bullied and the bystander* (New York, HarperCollins).

Emerson, R. W. (1860) *Essay on the conduct of life* (New York, Modern Library, Random House).

Hastie, R. (1997) *Disabled children in a society at war: a casebook from Bosnia* (Oxford, Oxfam International).

Kirk, R. (2003) *More terrible than death: massacres, drugs and America's war in Colombia* (New York, Perseus Books).

Machel, G. (2001) *The impact of war on children* (London, Hurst & Company).

Makdisi, J. S. (1999) *Beirut fragments* (New York, Persea Books).

Moses, L., Aldridge, J., Cellitti, A. & McCorquodale, B. (2003) *Children's fears of war and terrorism* (Olney, MD, Association for Childhood Education International).

Restrepo, L. (1999) *La novia oscura* [*The dark bride*] (New York, HarperCollins).

Taussig, M. (2003) *Law in a lawless land* (New York, The New Press).

Expressing the tradition in an educational context

Robert Jones

I was born in the borderlands of northeast Wales. My father was an Anglican (Church in Wales) and my mother a Welsh Calvinistic Methodist. My mother did not understand the Prayer Book and my father did not understand Welsh. So, at the point where they felt their children should go to Sunday school, they looked for a church to fulfil their purpose and out of a confusion of language, they tried the English Methodist Church and instantly found a spiritual home for the whole family. Since the age of three, I have been a part of the Methodist Church. I have been critical but never rebellious, which may be a fault. For the last twenty six years I have been a minister in the Church and for the last eight years I have been Chaplain of Southlands and Methodist/Free Church Chaplain to Roehampton University.

Southlands College is the last clearly identifiable Methodist college within mainstream higher education and, as Chaplain, I am to some considerable extent a custodian of the tradition. This means that for eight years, I have been asked, in a way that has never happened in the rest of my life, to explain what the Methodist Church is, what it means to be a Methodist and what it means to be a Methodist college. In local church ministry, the questions of identity are largely taken for granted. Even with the migratory tendencies of post-denominationalism, there is a gentle acceptance of history, doctrinal emphasis and cultural ethos. People stay in the Church if it feels right and if what is being said or assumed does not jar with personally held beliefs. In a college within mainstream higher education, the rules are different. Many simply ignore the foundational tradition until face to face with the keeper of the faith, and then the questioning begins.

Of course, many people have no idea about the Methodist Church but if they know something at all, they know that we are against things; that there is a sort of puritan spirit at large which requires caution. Notably, Methodists are seen to be against gambling and alcohol but this rapidly becomes the notion that they are essentially against anything that is fun or gives pleasure. It is a curious transposition, for this kill-joy reputation arises out of what was once a wholly admirable moral rectitude that allowed people to rescue themselves from poverty and squalor. The spiritual disciplines of Methodism were recognised as a social escalator for the aspiring working class. The recent publication of the *Oxford Dictionary of National Biography* has illustrated this vividly. It tells the story of one Marged ferch Ifan, born in the Snowdonia village of Beddgelert in 1696, who was both a harpist and wrestler. Her prodigious strength was legendary, accustomed as she was to wrestling two grown men to the ground at once without demur. She married the harpist Richard Morris (d. 1786), a man much slighter than herself, seemingly at her own proposal. It is said that she gave him two severe beatings. After the first, he married her ... and after the second he became a Methodist! It was, of course, a way out; a way of social as well as spiritual progression which offered a structure and discipline for life and a form of security not previously known. That has very much all gone. To join the social escalator, you need to join the Church of England, as Margaret Thatcher famously illustrated.

So over the generations, the Methodist Church has developed a distinctive culture that is hard to define though easy to recognise when it is embedded in the institution—the local church or in our case, the college. The evidence for this is set out below in a list that does not pretend to be exhaustive. The themes that I will describe are characteristic of the Methodist Church without attempting any claim that they are unique to our tradition. We share them with people of other Christian backgrounds and indeed sometimes other faith traditions. We also gladly acknowledge that men and women with no explicit faith will often endorse many of these themes in their relationships and daily life. What can be said is that these themes take a characteristic form in Methodist culture. They are not overtly theological, though each clause is undergirded by a distinct theological intention. Themes that are characteristic of Methodist culture will include the following:

- A warm and natural personal interest in each and every individual, irrespective of their role or status in the organisation.

- Practical care and thoughtfulness, shot through with generosity, in mutual relationships and in community service.
- A respect for authority, but a suspicion of 'hierarchy' or pomposity.
- A keen concern for justice and fairness, especially for those whose voice is least likely to be heard.
- A commitment to integrity, truth telling and high professional standards.
- A searching for ways of exercising responsibility towards the world's most disadvantaged people.
- A matter-of-fact spirituality, which integrates faith and everyday life, and which becomes focused in acts of worship which are relatively uncluttered, heartfelt and widely accessible.
- A good sense of humour which eschews hurtfulness and radiates esteem of others.

Even as I review these themes, they strike me as wholesome and attractive, as worthy and worthwhile; they are, to my mind, admirable and reflective of the Christian gospel which I want to espouse and which I want the Church of my belonging to reflect in its worship and its life. But can any institution—including an educational one—encapsulate the high principles of these objectives? Of course, the best we can answer is that it will be done; only imperfectly, but it can be done.

Methodism is a curious combination of two strands. On the one hand it is 'connexional', by which I mean that it is a highly centralised and unified structure of command and control with everything devolving back to Methodist headquarters. On the other hand, the interpretation of what it means to be Methodist is highly localised with many local and sometimes curious expressions of worship and practice. On another scale altogether, the Methodist Church has been a highly successful missionary enterprise throughout the world. Uniformity has not been a watchword but as a peripatetic preacher, I have visited Methodist churches all over the world. Although what happens locally may vary hugely and sometimes be barely recognisable, there is something in the ethos which makes these communities instantly identifiable as Methodist and gatherings of soul-mates with whom I feel entirely at home. Now it is that kind of ethos that we must attempt to establish within the life of the college. This begs two questions: how is this done and why should it be done? We address each in turn. How do we nurture the essence of the tradition in the life of an higher education college so that it makes a distinctive contribution to the whole university? It is important to say that there is no simple grand strategy, and even if there were, I don't believe it could work. What I offer in the following paragraphs is a summary of all that I have inherited, attempted to understand and make effective about our situation as the last solely Methodist presence in the higher education sector in the United Kingdom:

1. An architectural expression of our tradition. When I arrived, a brand new Southlands College was being built on a new site. It had been thought about and planned with the utmost care and now seven years after its opening, it has been fascinating to work in and grow into a suite of buildings that were planned with a theological purpose. There are many interesting details but I emphasise just two. First, the chapel is a circular building built to accommodate sixty people. It

has an extraordinary acoustic and works well with three people, splendidly with thirty and quite amazingly with one hundred and twenty. It is situated close to the main entrance to the college so that everyone who visits cannot fail to be aware of this centre of spiritual nurture that, by its existence and positioning, declares the honouring of faith and the spiritual journey. Second, the college itself, though architecturally modern and clean-cut, is built in classic collegiate style around a quadrangle (or cloister) but with one major difference to most monastic-style colleges and it is this: there are four open corners which means that when you are in the centre of the academy, you are constantly and visually aware of the world outside and anyone can come in (at least in theory) and anyone can get out (which is true in practice). This says we are an inclusive community with an articulate care for the world outside.

2.   An attempt at vernacular chapel worship. The gathered community of 'the chapel' comprises not one but several congregations in the course of seven or more services of worship each term-time week. Students and staff come from a variety of church traditions and none. The aim, then, is to create a form of worship that reflects the context—the academy, the congregation—a dolly mixture, and the college tradition—to be true to the Methodist heritage. We endeavour to synthesise a form of worship in a contemporary vernacular style within which everyone will recognise something of their own past experience but no-one in the first encounter will find a perfect glove-fit. For some, over a period of years, it becomes a perfect glove-fit but that is a happy by-product. Differences tend to be clearest in matters of music, liturgy, prayer style and participation:

(a)   Music can be tremendously divisive and we try to avoid this. Worship songs and traditional hymns tend to provide the polarities but there is a rich spectrum in between. Many students are enthusiastic about praise songs even if they do not particularly hold that theology. We involve students in the planning of worship and the choice of music whilst encouraging as much diversity as we can and regularly including the great hymns of the tradition. Musicians gather every week to form a scratch band but with a quality of playing that is often inspirational. After several years, we have developed a local repertoire but also try to stay up to date.

(b)   There is an ocean of good contemporary liturgy available and we try to use a range of sources. Our worship is structured but with a kind of laid-back formality. 'Experience' is a strong emphasis in Methodism. Much traditional worship is essentially cognitive but we try to address both sides of the brain. This acknowledges that unless the gospel truth is also received imaginatively, the individual is unlikely to integrate it within the whole person.

(c)   Prayer style is again a point of debate. The Methodist Church includes formal liturgical prayer and a vivid extemporary approach. We attempt to stay in touch with both in a creative contemporary way. It is worth noting, however, that the great extemporary tradition was informed by scripture and hymns committed to memory which provided a rich treasury of image and language. That is now largely lost so we have to find new ways of helping people to configure their prayers meaningfully where ardour does not over-whelm comprehensibility.

(d) Participation is essential to our style, not just in song and word but also in dynamic liturgical action, puppetry, dance and drama. We recognise the gift of a very talented congregation and over a number of weeks we aim to include every possible opportunity to enrich our overall experience.

3. An honouring of the spiritual quest and value in all members of the college. Members of all universities today come from a great variety of faiths and none. We articulate clearly our respect for faith of whatever background and a valuing of each individual's spiritual journey. Our chapel is a protected quiet space, not included in timetabled lectures or rehearsals. On a daily basis, a range of people come to be quiet, to reflect and to pray.

4. Self-conscious continuity. From a student perspective, colleges are annually changing communities. We realised that we would not carry forward the good traditions if we left it to chance. The majority of residents are first-years, who are clustered together in flats. Each first-year flat has one continuing student, specially commissioned to offer reassurance, pastoral care and guidance—especially in the first few weeks of the academic year. This group of continuing students form a powerhouse for activity and well-being in the college. They are trained in a programme devised and arranged by the chaplains and they are the student bearers of the college ethos and tradition from one year to the next. It is not foolproof but it does have a real effect.

5. Student-owned social projects. The chaplaincy operates a range of social projects, many of them with an international dimension that involve a broad cross-section of students throughout the college and the university. In Methodist terms, it is a reminder of John Wesley's dictum, 'there is no holiness that is not social holiness'. We offer the opportunity for students to be involved with some of the big issues of our day and to consider seriously, appropriate human responses to a divided and needy world. It is by these and other means that we try to establish an open and inclusive college community that honours the spiritual, has a contemporary feel, yet remembers the past into the present and the future and earths the individual's quest for meaning in the real world. Which brings us to the second question: why is it important to identify the tradition and ethos of the Methodist Church within the life of the college? I am making the personal assumption here that it is important, and I do this with an ever-increasing conviction. What we offer is different and distinctive. Methodism, along with all the mainstream denominations in the United Kingdom, comes from the Catholic tradition. We can trace a direct line of descent via Henry VIII and as such we are part of the main western tradition of the Christian world community. We give ascent to the principal creeds and rites of the church and would claim to be broadly mainstream in a Trinitarian theological understanding. Yet no-one entering a Methodist church or a Methodist college would mistake it for the Catholic or Anglican equivalent. It is no mistake to say we emphasise our non-conformity in this regard. This is not belligerent or whacky; indeed, quite the

opposite. There is often an air of worldly normality to the point where we are even sometimes accused of being dull. How does this work out?

The Methodist Church operates with a non-hierarchical structure. Of course, some people carry heavier responsibilities than others; that is the nature of any large organisation, but the Methodist Church operates with a principle of equivalence— that every person has the right to be heard and to influence the process of the Church. Universities, of course, are essentially hierarchical institutions and that can create some interesting tensions, but the principle of equivalence remains an important marker for acknowledging every member of the college. The Methodist Church is concilia in governments. Councils and committees also operate in universities and colleges but with varying degrees of effectiveness. The undergirding principle here is that of conferring. Decisions, wherever possible, shall be made through consultation—collegiately! This takes time and requires the goodwill and commitment of all college members, which is not always willingly given. As has already been noted, Methodism is an inclusive Church. John Wesley famously claimed, 'the World is my parish' and the early Methodist movement marched freely across boundaries to establish its particular missionary message and to draw all who would into the Methodist family. One description of social scientists would classify Methodism as both associational and inclusive. In practice this meant prospective 'members' were considered more for their intention than for the fine detail of what they believed. In the college context this means an easy acceptance of college members whatever their background, provided only that they accept the premise that they are part of a living community and to a greater or lesser extent this requires their commitment to make this community work. (In our case about twenty percent of the student community is Muslim.)

At its core, the Methodist Church believes that the love of God can change lives and do that to the uttermost. The unpacking of that simple sentence would take volumes but suffice it to say that in the life of a university college, this involves trying to provide the best environment in which staff and students may thrive and flourish. This sometimes means talking with a particular individual and working out just what might be possible for her or him and what needs to be done to make that achievable. This is slow, time-consuming and small-scale work but it influences the whole community. Of course, I can hear the chorus that says 'so what?'—not one of the conditions and criteria I have outlined above is unique or even unusual. What I am suggesting is that this particular selection of aims, objectives and methods combines within the human reality of a living tradition to create a distinctive and enhancing teaching and learning community.

Notes on contributor

Robert Jones is a Methodist Minister, Chaplain of Southlands College, Roehampton University, UK, and Higher Education Chaplaincy Co-ordinator for the Methodist Church.

Additional reading about Methodism

Craske, J. & Marsh, C. (Eds) (1999) *Methodism and the future* (London, Cassell).
Marsh, C. *et al.* (Eds) (2004) *Unmasking methodist theology* (London, Continuum).

The birth of a faith school in the post-Dearing era: asking questions and consultation, and getting things done

Howard Worsley

> God does not die on the day when we cease to believe in a personal deity, but we die on the day when our lives cease to be illumined by the steady radiance, renewed daily, of a wonder, the source of which is beyond all reason. (Hammarskjold, 1964, p. 64)

Factors in the environment

In an era that has seen a considerable drop in Anglican Church membership and attendance, Lord Dearing's review of Church of England schools made a considerable, not to say, surprising impact. This impact was, as could be perhaps expected, within the voluntary faith schools sector—and, interestingly, beyond. The factors that brought about the presentation of Lord Dearing's review *The way ahead* (2001) are multiple. However, it can be asserted that parental choice and published league tables were beginning to highlight schools that were successful and identify those that were comparatively unsuccessful. Oversubscription at some schools made it clear that public perception favoured the ethos of church schools and that demand was growing for greater provision to be made for more church/voluntary aided secondary schools to match the steadily popular church/voluntary aided primary schools. However, what was less certain was the public's *actual* attitude to the faith environment. Additionally, parties hostile to the voluntary sector in English schooling expressed doubts as to the value of denominational education. For example:

- was and is religion more of a cause for division than a means for global unity in the post September 11 world?
- would an Islamic faith school operate in a manner similar to a denominational Christian foundation school?

The start of the questioning

It was into this arena that *The way ahead* (Dearing, 2001) was launched, showing the fruits of widespread consultation between Church and schools, between state and the general public. It confidently asserted that 'Church schools stand at the centre of the Church's mission to the nation' (2001, p. 2) and offered the statistic that more children attended church/faith schools than the combined national population that attended church. The Report also offered the Church an opportunity to own and develop its existing schools and create new ones. For those of us involved in both church and education, it was a welcome challenge. But it also raised many questions:

- Were Church schools a mission field—or did this show a propagandist attitude to education that could verge towards religious abuse? (Layzell, 1999);
- Did the Report reopen the issue about separation of Church and state—a repudiation of Coleridge's call in the nineteenth century for a division to be made between national education and religion? (Coleridge, 1830);
- Was the need for an understanding of both Christian and a more general spirituality a feature in the demand for church schools?
- Was the public demand for more Church/voluntary aided education a form of inverted hypocrisy that said 'we want your ethos but not your faith?'
- Were voluntary aided and controlled schools being seen as a means whereby the public could deselect and so exclude certain types of children?
- In other words, was the selection procedure necessary to maintain the ethos of an aided school being used to deepen the rifts in society rather than heal them?
- Indeed, did questions of this kind indicate the evolution of a post-Christian spirituality in the twenty-first century?

From a church perspective, there was also a highly pragmatic question: did attendance at a church aided school have a positive or a negative influence on the religious attitude of the children who attended it? Recent research was ambiguous (Francis, 1996, pp. 48–49) and was the cause for some believing that Church of England education could be counterproductive. It could be seen to potentially be a means of inoculation, preventing pupils from coming to a personal faith later in life by giving them a small dose earlier in life.

Action taken: getting started and asking more questions

In the Diocese of Southwell (in the city and county of Nottinghamshire), we had been aware of the Dearing Report as it was prepared. We had had representatives on one of the subcommittees that had fed into the final paper. We had researched all the diocesan primary and secondary church aided and controlled schools and we had become aware of the central issues necessary for church schools to flourish. The schools wanted a closer link with their parish churches but they also demanded that the relationship be reciprocal and accountable. The demands went further to ask that priests should have it in their job description to support their local church/voluntary schools and that they should be adequately trained to do so. At the same time, it was becoming apparent that the City of Nottingham Local Education Authority (LEA) was not performing well in the national league tables for schools. Even so, it was a surprise when the Director of Education for Southwell Diocese was approached by the Director of Education for Nottingham City LEA to discuss the possibility of taking over an existing comprehensive school, with a view to it becoming a VA school.

At that time it was not apparent what this would entail but the mood in the Diocesan Board of Education (DBE) was encouraging. The proposal was debated and it was immediately apparent that the school in question, Wilford Meadows School, was on a prime site, near the River Trent. Wilford Meadows had been so named because it was established to attract pupils from both sides of the river, both urban and suburban-based. The vision to sustain the education of the pupils from both communities had never been fully realised, despite the vigorous attempts of the education authority. By the time the Diocese was consulted this visionary establishment had fewer than 100 pupils on its books. It was becoming a financial drain on the City LEA, despite the quality care being offered. This initial and tentative enquiry by the LEA to the DBE opened up a world that had as yet not been charted by the Church in Southwell Diocese. It was to challenge and stretch the thinking of the theologians, educationalists and practitioners at every level in the Church of England. The first question asked was simple enough:

1. Will the Church take risks in education?

At one level it was attractive to the Church to be asked to meet a public demand for more Church/faith secondary school places. It had seemed that the Church had not been a key player in educational affairs, and the notion that the Church could be part of fulfilling a stated need seemed appropriate. It was novel to have a working proposition that engaged educational and theological thought and drew on current practice and sociological trends. Some felt that this was an opportunity for the Church to show a commitment to the inner city. There was also an exciting possibility: whereas parental choice was deselecting more able pupils from certain comprehensive schools, this was an opportunity for the Church to establish a truly comprehensive school—one that created a situation appealing to pupils from different social strata.

This beautiful site, valued by various ecologically-minded societies, where birdsong could be heard within a mile of the city centre, was available for redevelopment.

The matter had to be discussed thoroughly, for at another level, this was a worrying proposal:

- Who could say that the Church could turn the school around?
- Whatever the Dearing Report said, should the Church *really* be involved in education?
- What financial commitments might be necessary? The reality was at this time that the Diocese was cutting back on its expenditure with a freeze on all clergy posts and a reduction of lay ones.

As the discussion went on, another question now began to be heard:

2. Can the Church deliver in education?

It became apparent to the DBE that widespread consultation was required at every level:

- with the LEA, with the community of the Meadows (in the City LEA);
- with the community of Wilford (in the County LEA);
- with the local churches and faith centres;
- with local councillors;
- and with the Bishop's Staff.

Building a team and planning what to do

In order to facilitate this process, a subcommittee was set up that had delegated authority from the DBE and which was required to report back to both the City LEA and the Bishop's Staff. As vice chair of the DBE, I was asked to chair this small group, which included the Diocesan Director of Education, the head teacher of another City VA secondary school, and other individuals familiar with LEA and Church politics or with wider financial experience. From the start it was clear that this was a group of positive activists, people who had the powerful combination of faith, partnership and hard work. In the early days of our meetings we drew up a list of tasks which included conducting a feasibility study, setting up consultancy meetings, exploring funding possibilities and communicating to the various agencies. It was essential that the group should appoint a project officer for the task, as time was already pressing on the group's outcome. The members were mainly busy professionals, offering voluntary services in their spare time. In the meantime the City LEA appointed its own project officer whose efficiency and administration was of high quality and who was demanding a similar response from us.

However, money was a key issue. The Diocesan Synod had granted no money for the consultation process and the DBE had allocated all its available capital to other projects or got it locked in reserved accounts. Only some complex negotiations and strongly-worded letters released the promise of £10,000 from the DBE to pay for the project officer. This was money from the next year's budget but with it we were able to make a suitable appointment.

This early experience of being without funds was a salutary reminder to the group, one that caused us to feel isolated and abandoned by the larger institutions whilst investing prime time and energy into the project. The experience of having a total lack of money whilst playing a game of high stakes was the first of several and it had the result of firming our resolve. Once the project officer was in post, a timeline was set up and adhered to. The group's task was now to monitor the officer and support him in his work. The timeline, drawn backwards, ended in the Schools Organisation Committees (SOC) for both the City of Nottingham LEA and the Nottinghamshire County LEA. Before that we had to offer presentations and hold public consultations, demonstrating our willingness to listen and to respond to the feasibility study.

Building trust: consulting and working with stakeholders

The paperwork and procedure for all this was done alongside the LEA and it seemed that part of our task was to assure them that the DBE would deliver, that our intentions were educational and not evangelistic. Looking back, we note the warmth of the LEA as it began to trust our commitment to providing places for the children from the Meadows and for children from other faith communities. What was more complex was the insistence by ecclesiastical bodies for information to be made available as and when they demanded, with little interest in how we were to achieve our objectives. It seemed that the partnership with the LEA was more supportive than the partnership with the Church.

Looking back, we also note that the process of public consultation was where we won the battle for people's trust. Being accessible to community activists, answering questions as to the new school's ethos, assuring potential parents of our joint commitment to the Meadows and to Wilford, meant that the tide of suspicion towards the Church began to change. I can remember a seminal moment when an outspoken young man from the Meadows directly challenged me as to my commitment to the urban poor in that area. Whatever my response, he seemed to accept my answer as being that of the Church's. At the end of the meeting he bought me a pint. He recalls that standing there with 'a vicar' (I was wearing a dog collar) and talking football and education was when he knew the new school would become a reality. In due course, he became one of our first 'temporary shadow governors'. He was later employed to network the primary schools in the Meadows and to assure them of the value of the new school. Needless to say, the period of consultation came and went, public notices were removed and the advent of the new school was widely supported. This, of course, was just the beginning.

Moving forward

As has been noted, we now had to set up a temporary governing body in order to usher in the new school. I was persuaded to stay on as the new Chair of Governors, and our previous working party handed over the responsibility (retaining a monitoring role if required). The composition of this governing body was statutory but we went to great lengths to find people who were not only representative but who had the necessary skills and time available. The resultant group showed the full range of diversity in its mixture of gender, ethnicity, skills and geography. For myself, this was one of the most interesting groups I have ever worked with. And this was just as well, because our tasks were multitudinous. We had to draw up legal documents, draw up the fine print of the admissions policy, write statements (concerning ethos, equal opportunity, etc.) and then we had to establish the funding streams and available revenue. Then there were the practical tasks like naming the school and finding the logo and designing the school uniform.

We called the school the Nottingham Emmanuel School (NES) because we felt that such a name reflected our belief that God was with us and that this new school was unashamedly a school with a Christian foundation. We spelt this out with our LEA partners and multifaith supporters. We came to realise that a specifically Christian spiritual ethos in which the other faith traditions were hosted by an Anglican framework was crucial to our overall purpose. If pupils wished to come to this school, they would need to honour such an intention. Put in these terms, without any tribal postulation or conversionist ideology, the surrounding community respected our identity. Our ongoing good relationships with the LEA now began to bear fruit. The LEA had thought ahead and budgeted that NES should have the money to appoint a head teacher and a part-time administrator during the fallow year. Our next task, therefore, was to proceed to appoint the head teacher. The advert was worded carefully:

> The Diocese of Southwell has been given a unique and exciting opportunity of starting a new Church Secondary School from scratch in an existing building.

We stated that governors were seeking a person with a 'clear Christian commitment' and one who also had 'a commitment to the highest standards of achievement for all'. The advertisement drew considerable interest and over 50 applications, somewhat bucking the trends for other faith/voluntary school headship posts. Maybe it was the visionary and entrepreneurial nature of the new job or maybe it was the emerging confidence that was felt following the publication of the Dearing Report. In the event we narrowed the field to an extremely strong cohort of secondary educationalists and appointed our head teacher. He was an existing secondary VA head who was willing not only to move house, family and job to take on the new challenge, but to take a cut in salary. As a head teacher he had a reputation for forthrightness and energy, stemming from a strong faith position. His appointment brought in a new phase for NES; and with it, the third question:

3. How can a new VA faith school gain credibility?

We have often joked that NES is not a new start school but a 'born again' school. In other words, the school was not simply a project of turning an old school around, using new staff, new resources and a facelift to the building. Maybe it would have been easier to re-enter the funding streams had it been so. What we were, was a completely new (born again) school, rising from the ashes of a school that had previously existed. All the pupils from Wilford Meadows had long since been re-allocated (about fifty of them) and NES was about to start life by gestating with a year's existence in shadow in which to build its new image, attract staff and attract pupils.

The head teacher planned ahead, working out what structural work should be done as the school grew, a year group at a time. In terms of the staff team, it was decided that we would start with high-quality and experienced people, who would develop into taking on senior posts at a later date. It was felt that the earlier appointment of deputy heads would be of value—even during the fallow year. Other needs were also identified. Who would be the person who would market the school in the Meadows and in the City and County, and in the Church? Much of this fell into the natural remit of the head teacher, but he needed more support. His felt needs were more than the LEA had budgeted and the Diocese had again budgeted nothing towards structural support. The governors, all new and visionary, were active in their subcommittees of pupil and personnel, curriculum and planning and also in working towards resolving transport issues and building a potential new road into the school. From where was the support to materialise?

As we became more familiar with the funding issues, it was a shock to realise that the Department for Education and Skills (DfES) had not put any budget provision aside for the new school because it did not even realise we existed. Fortunately, our new governing body was made of stern material and, far from being fazed, it began to plan on a budget that we did not have—at that point. Our list of needs and desires was lengthy. The head teacher wanted to appoint two new deputies partway through the fallow year. He wanted to appoint a part-time person to network the Meadows schools and to maintain the profile of NES, the school that was as yet invisible. He wanted to appoint a funding director to get us in touch with new funding streams coming online. To some governors this was exhausting. They lived in boundaried financial worlds where the greatest sin was to step outside budgetary provision. To work with someone who did not acknowledge the sufficiency of that provision was deeply stressful. To other governors this was confusing. They lived in more limited worlds where they had never had responsibility for large sums of money and so could barely comprehend the issues before them.

My own role and ethical questions

To myself, as a theological educator, there remained the deeply complex issues of living in the 'now and not yet' with the poorly educated and the sophisticated, with the important and the urgent. I was motivated at a very deep level by the vision of bringing an inclusive comprehensive education to a place that had been less privileged. I felt the power of my faith perspective working alongside social action and visionary education. However, in terms of finance, the whole project was in danger of being sabotaged by inadequate funds. It did not seem to be sufficiently owned by the sponsoring institutions. Was the answer to tread the precariously ethical route of spending what we did not have because the hand that held the purse had not understood our needs? Was the answer to grin and bear it, to pull in our belts and hope for the best? In the event, seeing that our new head teacher was ploughing forward, intent on making the school a success, I had the task of both supporting his vision and tempering his effect. To find money and to give him the Church support he so desperately desired, I had to create a bid to unlock capital reserves from the DBE. At a key moment in the life of the school, whilst it still did not actually exist, Southwell DBE released £100,000 which was immediately used to paint the building, create new signs, build a buffer of capital and, most importantly, show that the Church was owning the project. And it worked! The advertising, leafleting, consulting and printing of high-quality brochures yielded a return. The school was oversubscribed for year one. One hundred and eighty children streamed through the school gates at the beginning of the new school year in 2002. The sixty places reserved for Meadows children were all taken. This ushered in our current question:

4. Will the new VA school survive?

The future is the same for everyone: it is uncertain. But there are new funding streams and new means of making things happen. Our school has now welcomed its third year intake and is oversubscribed. What will our future goals be? Do we survive in the future by attracting sufficient pupils and keeping the books balanced? Or is survival to be measured in terms of maintaining a Christian ethos that adequately values pupils from different social strata, different credal backgrounds and different abilities?

Our ongoing efforts in running the school are certainly only maintained because of our commitment to our Christian ethos. It seems that 'post-Dearing' there are new opportunities for idealism in what can sometimes seem like the tired circles of secondary education. There are many teachers who are looking to make a difference by investing themselves in young people. Maybe the biggest question is whether the Church can rise from the back foot and embrace such an opportunity. In the case of our school, the Church has ultimately risen to the challenge financially and organisationally, albeit for the front-row players it has always seemed reluctantly. Authentic spirituality that offered commitment to the public, the Church, the LEA and children was high-risk.

In 2005, I took on the post of Director of Education for the Southwell Diocese. I am ever more mindful of the difficulties in setting up new ventures. My current questions revolve around how voluntary/faith schools are to be distinctive within contemporary culture; and how we can find a particular spirituality that is authentic, effective and replicable. Once that is clarified, can it be measured? Is spirituality something that we should attempt to benchmark within education? Should all schools reflect the secularising form of spirituality noted by Watson (2001) in her overview of Ofsted inspections? Or might there be a resourceful form of religious spirituality that should be developed in voluntary/ faith schools? Clearly, the questions are ongoing and endless; but they must be seen as a help to action, not as a hindrance, and as a means of finding, exploring and maintaining our sense of wonder—renewed daily—that *makes things happen.*

Notes on contributor

Revd Dr Howard Worsley is currently Director of Education for Southwell Diocese in the Church of England. He was previously Director of Studies in a theological college. He is an on-going researcher into how children articulate religious and spiritual experience.

References

Coleridge, S. (1830) *On the constitution of the Church and nation* (London, Routledge & Kegan Paul).

Dearing R. (2001) *The way ahead: Church of England schools in the new millennium* (London, Church House Publishing).

Francis, L. (1996) *Drift from the churches* (Cardiff, University of Wales).

Hammarskjold, D. (1964) *Markings* (London, Faber & Faber).

Layzell, R. (1999) Pastoral counselling with those who have experienced abuse in religious settings, in: G. Lynch (Ed.) *Clinical counselling in pastoral settings* (London, Routledge).

Watson, J. (2001) OFSTED's spiritual dimension: an analytical audit of inspection reports, *Cambridge Journal of Education*, 31(2), 205–219.

A 'tale of two cultures'—reflections on a dialogical study of a Jewish and a Catholic secondary school

Lynne Scholefield

I begin these reflections with some tales. In these you can hear the voices of some staff and students from two schools in England; Mount Sinai and St. Margaret's, one Jewish secondary school and one Catholic. These voices can be heard because, during some research in the late 1990s into the culture of the two schools, I carried out interviews and asked people for their views. The processes in which I was engaged during this research seem to me to be very like 'dialogue' although there was no formal dialogue going on between the two schools. I will be discussing what 'dialogue' means and how I used dialogical approaches in qualitative research. Perhaps what I have discovered about one particular Jewish school and one particular Catholic school will stimulate dialogue about education, faith and faith-based schools.

1. Some tales

The first voices come from Mount Sinai, a voluntary aided Jewish Technology College. That means it is a fully state-funded, mixed school for students aged 11–18,

Years 7–13. Here is the story as Ruth, a teacher, told it to me and then as the Year 13 and Year 11 students saw it.[1]

Ruth: King Hussein? That was the head's idea, just a brilliant idea, just cheek, *chutzpah*,[2] total *chutzpah*. They were discussing who they'd ask (to open the technology wing) and one of them said, 'Let's ask King Hussein. Ha! Ha! Ha!'. So they did and he said, 'Yes' and it was wonderful, it was absolutely wonderful. I mean I was proud to be there.

Lynne: What did you do?

Ruth: Cried. (loud laughter)

Lynne: What happened?

Ruth: He came, we had a song; he came and spoke. Actually the worst thing about that whole time was the sound system. He spoke to the kids very movingly and you couldn't hear it.

Lynne: Did you meet in the Sports Hall?

Ruth: Yes we all came down there, assembled in the Sports Hall. He marched on; the usual school things, songs and a presentation and then he spoke to the children for a long time without notes. I would say for quite a length of time and it appeared to be from the heart. It was obviously to do with children, they are all children wherever they come from and we should be working towards harmony and peace for the children and it was just lovely, the whole thing, the whole idea. What it did was to make, you know, Arabs human, more than anything else.

Lynne: Was there a lot of conversation among students about it?

Ruth: Oh yes. And some of the parents objected very strongly to the visit going ahead. Some parents claimed that it was a threat to the children because of the security aspect, very practical things, hot air going around. But the children were very much involved. It's something I don't think they will ever forget. Certainly I won't and I don't think any staff will. It was a privilege to be there.

David: Who would have thought, four or five years ago that an Arab, I mean a Muslim Arab, would come to a Jewish school. It would have been unthinkable, you know. In that way I thought it was very special. It was a shame that nobody could hear him. (Laughter)

Melissa: I couldn't see him, to be honest. He flew himself in, in his helicopter, landed in the playground, in the field over there. We all waited in the hallway and there was, like, special pupils were chosen to stand in front of him or open doors or whatever. He is very, very tiny. I never expected him to be so short. I couldn't see him at first, all I could see was pupils walking round and then there was this little guy and it was him.

Lynne: And he spoke to you?

David: He spoke; we could hear a few lines but nobody could tell what he was saying, not the details. I never actually got to speak to him but it was just nice to think he made the effort to come to the school.

Emma: There were a lot of mixed feelings about it though, weren't there?

David: I know a lot of people outside the school, more religious, you know, not extremist, but more religiously inclined people. They thought this bloke, you know, like (pause) he started war, you know, 20 years, 30 years ago and now, look how many Jews he killed then but now he wants to (words unclear). A lot of people were anti. I thought it was great.

Lynne: There are very few photographs up anywhere of the visit.

David: It was very short and sweet ... There was a video, they taped it all but I don't know where it's gone ... There wasn't much opportunity to take pictures of him because he was only here half an hour. He literally came down, came out, made his speech and went straight back up again.

Jane: I met him. He arrived from a helicopter and we had to show him around the technology wing and he came in and the press were just taking photos and he came over to see what I was doing and I was about to put something in the kiln and it was just an amazing atmosphere, just all of a sudden.

Jo: I think it was really good because not many people get a chance to meet a king of any country. I think it was brilliant that the school had something like that.

The head teacher commented to me about the visit, 'It encapsulated the idea that almost anything is possible, that's what was exciting about it, so it kind of summed up what the school is trying to be about'. There are lots of other things in this extract which also typify for me what that school was like such as the use of Yiddish, the strong connections between the school and the local Jewish community, the ever-present concern about Israel, and the very positive feelings which many students have about the school.

Now some voices from St Margaret's, also a voluntary aided mixed secondary school for 11–18-year-olds, this time a Roman Catholic school. I asked everyone I interviewed to choose a symbol for the school and one teacher chose the doormat as her symbol:

> It was quite funny when it was introduced, 'Welcome to St. Margaret's', it says and everyone wipes their feet on it. It was really nice and bright when it first came and now it is quite tatty. Like the school, quite friendly, small, a bit tatty but okay.

Maria, the deputy head, chose a hand sheltering a flame. This is a caring image, a kind of embrace which people in the school try to provide for all. There have been five attempted suicides by students in the recent past and so the view of education in the school, Maria says, means 'preparing for death rather than life'. While I was talking to her on one occasion there was a phone call from a parent with heart problems whose daughter has kidney failure and whose son has leukaemia. 'Anything we can do', Maria said, 'let us know'. There is a tradition of St Margaret's as a *nice* school but Maria thinks that perhaps it is overprotective, not academically pushy enough.[3]

Another symbol I was given was a growing plant. Jennifer had been in the school for more than ten years. When I interviewed her she was a head of department and had witnessed a lot of change and 'movement towards growth'. She also said that despite some difficult changes there was a sense among the staff of underlying strength and camaraderie, an atmosphere that hasn't changed. That creative atmosphere had been noticeable from the first day Jennifer came to the school, 'I experienced it the moment I walked in the place, not very tangible; I just sensed something different, there's a consciousness, there's a perspective that simply adds something to the daily work'. Jennifer sums this up as 'duty, love and service, a sense of being there for others'.

> Jennifer: The way in which we deal with children's, uh difficulties, uh, traumas, a little lad whose dad died the other week and the way in which the school has contact with the home. I don't know, it might be normal everywhere, it's just, it's that awareness of need which I think is pretty important.
>
> Lynne: Yes. I'm getting a sort of sense from quite a lot of people that the way in which the school handles dying and death ...
>
> Jennifer: Oh Yes!
>
> Lynne: is something really quite important...
>
> Jennifer: Oh Yes! Absolutely!
>
> Lynne: for its identity.
>
> Jennifer: Absolutely! When I was hauled in here, 'cause I mean my dad was ill for years, because dad had died very suddenly that morning, there was an absolute competence in the way it was handled. You know, compassion but competence. I got home and the head rang because he was out that day so hadn't been there. That sort of thing. You know. Colleagues very, uh, easy is not the right word, but easy when dealing with you. Which makes, so there's no fear or embarrassment. And then Mass is offered so, you know, important things.
>
> Lynne: Because you've had pupils who've died?
>
> Jennifer: Oh yes we have. Oh gosh, yes. We've had a very difficult couple of years when three or four pupils died; one through a car accident, two through terminal illness and again the home–school partnership was important, you know, representation at the funeral, participation in preparing choirs, that sort of thing. So, yes, very important.

The Year 10 students were not able to name an image for the school but they agreed that whatever it was it would have to have lots of different parts to it to reflect the different aspects of the school. They mentioned the social life, the drama production, clubs after school where they can achieve a lot, lessons and the idea of community. 'This secondary school is quite small so everybody, sort of, not everyone knows each other but familiar with everyone ... knowing what everybody is like ... The symbol would have to be something to do with a family ... where we're known ... with the family tiffs'.

Several staff were not able to name a symbol for the school either but the theme of community came through in what they said. As one teacher put it, 'something that would represent a big group, a big community, you know, people higher up in the school getting on with people lower in the school'.

St Margaret's is not an academically high-achieving school, unlike many Catholic schools in Britain and America. It prides itself on its happy, caring atmosphere which values each individual and which encourages the celebration of diversity. I could go on telling tales from the schools about what wonderful places they are but I want to introduce some counter views, voices which tell a different story.

At Mount Sinai there are different understandings of what it means to be Jewish and so what it means to be a Jewish school. The head teacher and the Jewish Studies staff do not live in the local Jewish community. They are *frum* (Yiddish for 'religious' or 'orthodox' or 'observant') and some of the local people, including staff, governors and parents who are not *frum* find that their Jewish lives do not correspond to the messages being given by the school that Jews should be observant. A parent who works in the school told me that she felt 'the *frummers* tend to look down on us'. She keeps kosher at home but not when eating out. She goes to *shul* (synagogue) every week but she might drive there if it is wet.

This tension is symbolised by McDonald's. A Jewish teacher said to me:

> It isn't part of the school ethos to approve the non Jewish things they get up to such as going to McDonald's on a Friday afternoon. Of course we can talk about it but it is a game that is played, 'You shouldn't be going to McDonald's but we know you do'. Really they know I don't give a damn. That isn't what is important to me about being Jewish, but I've never said that and I wouldn't ever dream of saying it. If I was asked, 'Do you keep *kosher*?', I would say, 'No', but they never have; they wouldn't put me on the spot ... I think (in this area) it's much more relaxed, much more open, much more accepting of variety, much more tolerant and wants to see that tolerance reflected in the school but some of the structures in place don't reflect that ... 'Our Judaism isn't good enough', that is the subtext.

The head teacher's comments about McDonald's in a dissertation he wrote are interesting:

> Was there a difference between eating in McDonald's with your family at the weekend or on Friday after school while still wearing school uniform? ... Pupils in Year 8 felt strongly that the school had little right to a say in their lives outside school. All the Governors were of the opinion that the school clearly did have a right to react and that it should if pupils were eating non kosher meat while in school uniform. This view was even shared by Governors who themselves were in no way religiously orthodox. When the question was whether the school should therefore react to eating non kosher generally, there was however a different response. Outside school and outside uniform, some Governors, most noticeable the Parent Governors, felt that it was not the school's business. When presented with the dilemma that the school's message would then be, 'eating non kosher is forbidden only as long as you are wearing school uniform' they admitted the absurdity of this argument but none the less did not change their position! (Falk, 1996, p. 55)

So there is some resistance among students, parents and governors to the idea that Jewish values and learning should permeate all aspects of life. Differences of perspective are also a feature at St Margaret's. The school prides itself on the quality of the liturgies, the services which take place daily and to mark special occasions such as the beginning and end of the school year. There is a funded post of liturgy coordinator and the liturgies are very carefully prepared to make a connection between students' lives and Christian worship. Talking about the programme of worship in the school, the head teacher said:

We can share our joys and there have been times when we've had to share our sorrows as well and I think that is hugely important. When you touch people at that fundamental level then, you know, a lot of the other things you do assume a relative unimportance.

However when Year 12 and 13 students responded to a questionnaire item about the influences on their religious development, school liturgies came last out of nine possible influences. Only a quarter believe that senior students understand and accept the religious goals of the school.

2. The relevance of dialogue

I have been illustrating some of the differing views within each school about what it means to be a Jewish or a Catholic school. In much writing about faith-based schools these voices are never heard. Writing about Jewish or Christian education is often theoretical or prescriptive, and much of it is intended to inspire, but it often seems out of touch with actual school experience. For example, the Chief Rabbi in England, Jonathan Sacks, has repeatedly linked Jewish continuity with Jewish education, and *The Jewish Chronicle*, Britain's leading Jewish newspaper, regularly carries an advertisement for a charitable trust which proclaims 'Anglo Jewry's survival? The only proven way is by building more Jewish Day Schools'. St Margaret's diocesan bishop wrote that 'the Catholic schools in our Diocese will be places where gospel values will be proclaimed and lived and will offer to our fragmented society examples of integrity, compassion and commitment to social justice' (Murphy-O'Connor, 1996, p. 14). I do not want to argue with the sentiments being expressed; they are admirable and the claims may be true, but there is not really any evidence for them. Because relatively little research has been carried out into Catholic and, particularly, Jewish schools in Britain, and the lives and views of their students and teachers, I would argue that no one really knows. If there is to be a dialogue between the theories of Catholic education and the experiences of Catholic schools, and between the theories of Jewish education and the experiences of Jewish schools, then the voices from the schools have to be heard. The research that I did into the cultures of two particular schools was designed to amplify the sound of these little-heard faith-based school voices in order to contribute to an intra-Jewish and intra-Catholic dialogue about schools and education. In my thesis I held back discussion of the theoretical ideas about education within Judaism and Christianity until the end so that they could be heard in the light of the voices from the schools.

I saw my own role as a researcher involving a form of dialogue and I will explain here what I mean by the term 'dialogue'. Martin Buber (1958) wrote about an *I–Thou* relationship which was possible for someone to have with the natural world, with other persons and with God. This is a subject–subject relationship of openness, directness, mutuality and presence. Not only is dialogue a way of relating to other people, it is also, I think, a possible way of knowing. The feminist scholar, Donna Haraway (1991, p. 198), called this 'situated knowledges' where the object of knowledge is an active agent and the knower is engaged in a 'power-charged social relation of "conversation"'. This conversation or dialogue must involve both listening to, and telling, 'stories' which try to articulate our experience and how we see things. We are both speaking and listening in the presence of 'the Other' and it is important to find an approach which neither demonizes 'the Other' or treats 'the Other' as essentially the same as oneself. There is much interesting material which is relevant to this account of dialogue in writing about feminist theory, narrative theology in Judaism and Christianity, and in the theology of inter-faith dialogue.[4]

In the case-study research which I have discussed here, my own story played a significant part. I come from a background in religious education in Britain with a particular interest in the teaching of Judaism. When I began to work in a Roman Catholic College of Higher Education a few years ago I was not a Catholic. I found the experience interesting. I had a strong sense of being an outsider and this was at times uncomfortable but I was also aware that I was struck by things which 'insiders' took for granted; the dining room was called 'the refectory' (a Benedictine term) and there was a large chapel at the heart of the campus and of college life. I became conscious of things which Catholics seemed to do particularly well, such as handling death and dying.

Becoming a Catholic in 1993 made me officially an 'insider' in Catholicism although I have continued, to some extent, to remember my outsider perspective. It also developed my relationship with Judaism in several ways. Catholics are very involved in Christian–Jewish dialogue and, as a Catholic, I was somehow now 'licensed' to participate actively in that dialogue. In dialogue one somehow 'hears the other into speech' and both listening and speaking can be very powerful. Because dialogue is two-way, I not only learned about, and from, Judaism more deeply, I also discovered that I was finding my voice as a Catholic. This happened most vividly studying the Bible which, since I was now a Christian, was 'my book' too. In shared, interactive study of biblical and para-biblical texts with Jews, I drew closer to the texts themselves, to Judaism and to Christianity.

Going to Poland with a Jewish Studies delegation in 1994, I was the only Christian in the group; again an outsider. In the Jewish Museum in Warsaw there is an exhibition of items which survived from the Ghetto. We saw exercise books used by children in the days before they were sent to Auschwitz. These children would not have a future, they would not live to experience adult life, but it was still seen as important that they received education. One of the Jewish delegates summed up this commitment to education in those dreadful circumstances as 'the distilled essence of teaching'. Teaching and learning were a form of resistance to dehumanisation, an assertion of human identity where the human being, fully alive, is a studying human being.

Here was an idea of education which went far beyond the issues then raging in Britain about the National Curriculum. I began to wonder what Jewish schools in Britain were like. I became interested in knowing about their cultures, their traditions, their taken-for-granted ways of doing things. Meantime, I sometimes realised how quickly I had stopped noticing the Catholic particularity in the ways we did things in my own college. Some of the language, the traditions and the values had become my own; I had become more fully an insider. I was visiting a large number of Catholic schools where I also felt very much 'at home'. I became interested in what these staff and students would say about their cultures, their traditions, their taken-for-granted ways of doing things. I decided to study the culture of a Jewish and a Catholic school in the light of my experiences of Jewish–Christian dialogue.

This story about my changing relationships with Jewish and Catholic traditions is both a part of the research I have done and a result of the impact of this research on my life; reflexivity is part of the methodology I used. I was concerned to get students and teachers in the schools to tell their stories, and narrative issues are important in studying and writing about culture. I presented tales of the culture of St Margaret's and Mount Sinai in a way which enables each to be heard in its own particularity but in the presence of 'the Other': the researcher, the other culture, the voices beyond the school, and the listener or reader who is also invited into the dialogue. By moving backwards and forwards between Jewish and Christian material I try to maintain a fruitful tension between insider and outsider perspectives, never letting the cases become too familiar or too strange. In fact, within both schools there was also a real openness to 'the Other' within a stress on community and identity.

The importance of this openness for the future of Britain as a tolerant and safe place for many diverse people and cultures has grown in the years since the case studies were carried out. A new Pope has just been chosen, whose commitment to inter-faith dialogue is perhaps not as strong as his predecessor. Faith-based schools have a long history of understanding education as being about the formation of persons. I end with a number of questions which seem to me to arise from my dialogical study. What kind of persons are schools trying to form? How do schools handle the students who do not share the values the school is based on? How do faith-based schools, including Muslim schools, contribute to the common good?

Notes

1. The verbatim quotations are from transcripts of recorded interviews.
2. Leo Rosten (1968, p. 94) defines *chutzpah* as 'gall, brazen nerve, effrontery, incredible "guts"; presumption-plus-arrogance such as no other word, and no other language, can do justice to. The classic definition of *chutzpah* is, of course, this: *chutzpah* is that quality enshrined in a man who, having killed his mother and father, throws himself on the mercy of the court because he is an orphan'.
3. In several subjects, standards of achievement at GCSE (age 16+) are close to, or above, national averages but overall results are below national norms for maintained secondary schools.
4. For fuller discussion of this see Scholefield (2005, pp. 21–27).

Notes on contributor

Lynne Scholefield is Senior Lecturer in Theology and Religious Studies at St Mary's, Strawberry Hill, Waldegrave Road, Twickenham, TW1 4SX, UK.

References

Buber, M. (1958) *I and Thou* (2nd edn) (Edinburgh, T&T Clark).

Falk, A. (1996) *Developing a community school.* Unpublished M.Ed. dissertation, University of Warwick.

Haraway, D. (1991) *Simians, cyborgs and women* (London, Free Association Books).

Murphy-O'Connor, C. (1996) *The Catholic school—the church in the world* (Crawley, Diocese of Arundel and Brighton Schools Commission).

Rosten, L. (1968) *The joys of Yiddish* (London, Penguin Books).

Scholefield, L. (2005) Women knowing, women in dialogue, in: H. Fry, R. Montagu & L. Scholefield (Eds) *Women's voices* (London, SCM Press).

Interview

Helen Johnson

Jonathan is a second-year university student who is currently studying education. He volunteered for this interview after a group discussion about faith schools. He had attended a Church of England secondary school in Northtown and 'wanted to put some things straight'.

Issues around selection

Interviewer: I'm so pleased you've let me talk to you about Northtown Comprehensive School.

Jonathan: We don't know it as Comprehensive. It's just Northtown School. We try to forget the comprehensive bit ... it seems because it's kind of selective.

Interviewer: How is it selective?

Jonathan: Okay. To get into the school there's a point system and depending on the amount of people wanting to go there each year depending on points you needed. So, you'd get so many points for going to church for so many years. You'd get so many points for being regular in attendance. You'd get so many points if your parents were involved with the church. If they did extra things with the church with their own school. I'd get a few extra points because my brother was—and things like that. You know, if there's 300 spaces for the year and 500 people wanted to go, it might be a high point score. But one year there was 300 places and only about 290 people wanted to go, so there was virtually no points score required and there was a Muslim girl who got in the school, just because she didn't have to have any points, so she could get into the school.

Interviewer: But, you talked about regular church going. Was that checked up on?

Jonathan: Yeah. They had to sign a declaration saying—they didn't lie because the nature of the job—they used to get people trapped this way because you know, generous statements but the—usually—it was checked up on one school.

Interviewer: Did you go to a faith primary school?

Jonathan: Church of England Primary School, just a local one which was quite good. My brother went there. I went there. It did okay for us. It wasn't fantastic, having my experience now but it was good enough.

Interviewer: But was it an expectation to get into a faith secondary school since you'd been to a Church of England primary?

Jonathan: Not necessarily. They'd take Catholic people. Most primary schools in my area were Church of England anyway. So it didn't really matter. Obviously more people went to Northtown School because it had the right ethos and ... teachers were local. You'd get areas where a lot of the governors of one school would go to the same church as one of the higher teachers in the school, so they'd probably have more of an intake.

Reasons for going to a faith school

Interviewer: Can I ask why did you go to that school?

Jonathan: Well, one of the main reasons was because my brother was there and my parents knew it was a good school. I think my parents sent my brother there because it was a good school and we didn't go to church deliberately to get into the school, we went to church because my Mum made us. My Dad didn't bother going. But my Mum went to church, so we had to go to church as well and then, once we kind of got into the school then you know, we used to get to do other things as well because we got into sailing and that was on a Sunday morning. So by the time I got into Year 8 at the School, I'd virtually stopped going to church. I don't believe in God myself. My brother doesn't either. My Dad we don't really know—we never really asked him the question. He has never answered despite all the asking, he just won't answer it.

Interviewer: But you mentioned that it was a good school. What do you think is meant by a good school?

Jonathan: Well it's got good academic results. The children that go there are generally very well behaved. It's got a high perception of a good school. Right where I live there are four or five council estates within the immediate area where I live and the schools, just up the road, we get a lot of intake from there. So the standards aren't as good. You get a lot more behaviour problems. My school is seen as a bit of a posh school, not overly posh but you know, if you went there you weren't the local normal person ... because it was six miles away, so it used to take me between half-an-hour to an hour on the bus to get there. Whereas if I went to a local one it was a 10-minute walk up the road.

Interviewer: Right. So it wasn't so much—here's a leading question. It wasn't so much the religious aspect of the school that was attractive or the fact that there was good discipline, good results.

Jonathan: Good discipline. Good results because of the religious aspect. Because people who generally go to church often are the people who are more involved at the primary school. You get parent/governors, stuff like that. And the parents that maybe go to the church with them often seem to take more of an involvement. That's how it was seen by the students there.

Interviewer: Again, this is a very difficult question but was it your perception that most people were coming from two parent families?

Jonathan: Yeah. It was a very white middle class, two parents—I did know some people that didn't have two parents, but not many. The majority were middle-class. Some less affluent people but it was hard to tell because—a good test is the school dinners' one. But I always had sandwiches and I kind of ate outside so I didn't really see that aspect. I never used the canteen. But towards the end they did introduce a payment card so that you wouldn't see who was getting free meals and stuff. But as far as I am aware most people were reasonably well off or you know, could afford a—like new blazers £40/50 and you'd probably have to get a new one every year because ... grew and there were kind of from specialist shops. You know, bottle green, special logo, rather than some of the sort of cheaper ones that are just general and you sew it on. Kind of the whole perception of it was a better school.

Interviewer: What was it like?

Jonathan: It was good. The teachers were generally good. They made you get on with the work. Quality of teaching—it was pretty good and a lot of people got good results. I personally got at GCSE 8—'A's, a 'B' and a 'C' which was quite good but not the best. My best mate got 9 'A*' and an 'A'. He revised, I didn't. I didn't have to work—I was lucky in the respect, I was top set for almost everything. I didn't have to do any work. I'd get the homework done on the bus in the way in. So I considered myself quite well academically. But, even the people that weren't as well off academically seemed to do all right. There was a good 5 A–C rate. I think 90-odd% or something like that. I'm not sure. You know, people used to compete, not individually but like they used to be compared with your year was doing against the year above or the year below and see who was doing better. The teachers used to make comparisons. They used to say, last year they were much better, you can do better.

Religion at the faith school

Interviewer: Once you were in, was there a lot of religion?

Jonathan: You used to have the yearly assemblies—I have to think about this. Once or twice a week, I actually can't remember. But there was religious aspects to that and in registration in the morning the teacher would say a prayer and do the notices and take the register. Some form tutors were more religious than others. It wasn't just the children that had to go to church. All the teachers had to be a member of the church as well and they were selected in that way. The two main requirements for teachers was they had to have a degree in the subject they were going to teach and they also had to be church-goers.

Interviewer: Any other overt signs of religion?

Jonathan: There was—every year, you'd go down to the centre of town for the Christmas stuff ... at Christmas you'd have the usual Carol Service but it was half the school because you couldn't fit everyone in the same building and you'd have your Carol Service. And you'd have to—every term you'd go for Communion. The Communion in the actual main assemblies every term, but also you'd have a formal Communion time where you'd go off to the chapel. There was a chapel as well. Religious education was compulsory. You had to do it at GCSE. So, and they're very keen on that. You even got setted in Religious Education. I was quite miffed because I was only in Set 2 and I was in Set 1 for almost everything else, apart from French. But they offered me to move up but I was always the argumentative one that—I didn't believe—I played Devil's Advocate with the teacher and wind them up, just to get them promoting—because one of the teachers I had, one of the arguments was, 'what evidence is there of God and things like that'. The Bible and I'd say, well that's a biased view written by believers so how's that evidence. Well, the Bible. Sometimes the teacher struggled on the theological arguments.

Being a devil's advocate

Interviewer: So what was the teachers' attitude to you as a devil's advocate?

Jonathan: Fine. Because as I was a good student they just saw me as promoting a conversation in the class. I had a bit of a reputation as a bit of a 'geek'. From some people I didn't mind. I didn't have many friends there but that's just me. I didn't get bullied really. The first year someone tried to pick on me but the school sorted it. They had a very strict bullying policy as well, you know. Anonymous bullying boxes, bullying was dealt with decisively and firmly. Sort of looking after the people. ... anonymous boxes if you needed to—... religious aspects.

Interviewer: But, I mean, you as the devil's advocate, yes, you weren't made to feel uncomfortable?

Jonathan: No, not at all. They realised—in every day lessons religion wasn't pushed. It was just like a normal school but you had the caring—but the pastoral support had a religious aspect. It wasn't—in your maths lesson it was just an ordinary maths lesson. English, ordinary English. It was just in religious studies I would just ... people that you not always agreed with what the teacher was saying and take it blindly. Which in a way they kind of appreciated because it promoted a discussion. There was a few of us like when they have the assemblies where you go for Communion, you used to go up in your forms and get the Communion. If you didn't take Communion you'd get a Blessing. So I started out doing that until I got brave enough to just stay in the seat. Some people just stayed in the seats if they didn't want to go and get a Communion or Blessing. You know, if they decided they didn't believe in God, whatever, they just stayed in the seat. And I kind of from Year 9 onwards I just stayed in my seat when the rest went up. So, the teachers didn't mind that. They understood that people make a choice. That's the whole—the way they understood it. The whole ethos of the Church, you get christened because that's your parents' choice to bring you up that way. And when it's your choice you get your baptism or confirmation or whatever it is. I didn't go through it because they didn't do that in my Church anyway because I'm United Reformed and they didn't have—you started taking Communion when you wanted to. Whereas the Church of England did and so, you know, they'd take people from Methodist, Church of England, United Reformed. As long as it was an Anglican religion then you know, it was all right for the school.

Interviewer: Right. So, you're not an Anglican?

Jonathan: No. Well, I'm—Anglican covers United Reformed, Church of England, so I'd come up as an Anglican but not a Catholic. So you know, again, I'm getting my terms mixed up. Yeah. Protestant, yeah. Anglican is Church of England, isn't it? Yes, I'm not an Anglican, I'm—I was christened a Methodist. Went to the United Reformed Church. Went to a Church of England primary school and the secondary school was Church of England. But they weren't pressures on us, you had the same beliefs in God. Or, you know, not necessarily ... you attended the church.

Interviewer: Did you enjoy this school?

Jonathan: Yeah, I enjoyed it. It was good and I felt like I was having a good time. I made some friends. Good education. I had a knee injury so I didn't do well at sports but you know, the swimming pool. So, I got to do the swimming all the time. I worked in the library instead of doing sports sometimes. So, I had a good time in school. I enjoyed it. Made friends, lots of facilities...

Interviewer: Right. Is it a fun place? Sounds fairly ...

Jonathan: No, it was fun. It wasn't—I might be showing it serious but it was fun, you know. It was like an ordinary school. The religion wasn't forced down your throat. It wasn't strict in that respect.

Indoctrination

Interviewer: You didn't feel you were being indoctrinated?

Jonathan: No, no, not in the slightest. It felt to me just like an ordinary school. I'd been to a Church of England primary school. It was like your standard comprehensive but they maintained—a lot of schools don't bother doing the daily acts of worship. At this school they did do prayer. The headmaster was a Reverend. We had a couple of other, three or four different other Reverends. Teachers of religion are often lay preachers or actual Reverends.

Interviewer: Was there a lot of religious pictures or symbols or—

Jonathan: Not really, no.

Interviewer: I mean, could you have walked into the school and not known that it was a Church of England School?

Jonathan: Yeah, quite easily. In the Hall you've got some of those paraphernalia up on the walls or on a table in the corner. Or, if you go to the school now, they've just built a brand new chapel right at the front with a big glass window and stuff, so you know that it is when you go there. But when I was there you could go in and it would be just like an ordinary school and it was just the way that—they seemed to have the Christian ethos of caring and—so it was like an ordinary school but with the religion that is required by law, up to a point. Well, you've got to do your daily worships, so we did. Even if it was just a prayer at the end of registration or something like that, then the teachers did it. The school policy was for them to do it.

Interviewer: So, it was very clearly a Christian school?

Jonathan: Yeah.

Interviewer: You mentioned a Muslim girl ...

Jonathan: Yeah, that was before my time. My brother told me about that. But that's when the points' score was so low. I can almost presume that she didn't have to do everything. Like I didn't have to do the Communion, so I didn't, because that was my choice. So you weren't forced sort of thing but you did have to do your Religious Education GCSE. But that wasn't kind of indoctrinating you into the viewpoint, that was just educating you into the different ways. We spent more time looking at different religions around the world than we did our own. So that was just a general religious education curriculum. Nothing—it wasn't too biased. Obviously, they would focus a lot more on the system they knew but they did give you a good general view point.

Interviewer: You mentioned the staff and the staff had to be practising Christians. What were the staff like?

Jonathan: Ordinary, general people. I have to say, white and middle class. I think—no Asian teachers.

Interviewer: Your school was always pretty white, was it?

Jonathan: Yeah. There's a couple of black people but well established. A lot of generations in. It was—more middle-class areas of Northtown tend to send kids there.

Overall experience

Interviewer: Overall, what would you say your experience of the school was like?

Jonathan: Good. I enjoyed it. Made friends. It's not scarred me for life. It's educated me. It's given me lots of opportunities because I might not have achieved as high in some of the other schools. If I'd gone to a local school I don't think I would have done as well because I wouldn't have had so many opportunities. And the expectations are high for everyone so that kind of encourages everyone to do as well.

Interviewer: What's your response to the accusation that church schools are socially divisive?

Jonathan: In that respect they are, yes, because your parents who go to church and send their kids to church schools are often the ones that take part generally. Parent/teachers—your PTA Committee and stuff at primary schools are often those people that tend, you know, that care more about their child's education and get more involved in it. And, I'm making a general statement. From how I see it, they're more likely to help you with your homework than the parent who is not really that interested in getting involved in your primary school. And the social divisiveness in respect that I didn't know many people, poor people at my secondary school. Whereas if you looked at other local schools you could see a lot of people living in council estates to the local schools. Whereas people travelled from quite a distance to Northtown Secondary even from out of the Borough, you'd get a few people getting bussed in.

Interviewer: Do you think that the admission process was such with the points system that people were selected on the basis of whether they would fit it on not?

Jonathan: Yes, in respect that they'd fit in because they were of the Christian ethos and they took part. But also, they fitted in because if you pick the people that go to church and make an effort and go through all the appeals process, you know, the points system and that, the rigid application then they are people that care about their education, so they are more likely to encourage their children to do well in the school and you'd get them to work and things like that. That's how it seemed to me at the time. I might have a slightly prejudiced view because that's the way I've been brought up, to see other parents—

Interviewer: You don't feel got at?

Jonathan: No.

Interviewer: I mean, would you send your own kids there?

Jonathan: It depends. Only because I don't believe in God and I don't know if I'd want to make my kids go to church. But, if the points level were low enough so that they didn't have to then, yeah. It was a good school. I had a good time there and you know, why not. I wouldn't want to send them to a school with a less good academic record. I knew people from my primary school who were just as clever as me and they went to other schools and they didn't do as well in GCSEs. It could be for a variety of facts but I think it's because I went to that school and I got the opportunity to go to that school.

Interviewer: You keep drawing a picture of a school that was academically achieving. But you also mentioned in terms of a pastoral care system but based on Christianity and caring and you didn't feel bullied or— there were processes that you could go through if you did feel bullied.

Jonathan: Any good school would have those kind of things but not necessarily with a Christian aspect. So it was a good school with Christian things. I suppose it's kind of additional to that but because of the Christian views probably what's caused them to do this. But I think if you get a look at the history of the school, I can't remember it all.

Interviewer: Are there any questions that I haven't asked you about Northtown School that you were expecting to answer?

Jonathan: Not really. I thought you might ask whether a lot of people end up changing their view about religion and stuff like that. A lot of people I knew there still are committed Christians and they … church and they do believe. A lot of people believe in God but they don't go to church. Don't have the time. Can't be bothered. And then, there's some like me but you know, decided it's not the thing for me. I don't personally believe in that.

Interviewer: But you feel informed?

Jonathan: Yeah, very informed. They gave us all the options and things like science. Science was taught in a scientific way. No religious bias to it at all. So it's just standard science. The religion didn't interfere with the teaching of normal subjects, in normal ways, so it gave you a fairly evenly balanced outlook on life and different subjects and things like that, I think.

Interviewer: I mean, would it be fair to say that from the way that you've described it, it sounds like essentially a grammar school rooted within the Christian tradition?

Jonathan: As much as I understand grammar schools. I thought—personally, I thought they'd been abolished years and years ago, everywhere. I didn't know. It was only until I came down here and started on the Primary Ed Course that I find out there are still grammar schools around.

Interviewer: But this is a school that sees the world through Christian eyes ... Is that fair to say?

Jonathan: Probably a little bit too much. It gives you a chance to see the Christian ethos and understand everything but it doesn't make you look at science as a Christian. It makes you look at science as a scientist. And then they encouraged you to use your Christian views as well. If you wanted to—in science we had discussions sometimes about the ethics involved in some science particularly, biology and I want babies and things like that. And genetic engineering. And they'd offer you know, the teacher would discuss all different points of view and they would make sure—they'd explain what the Christian view would be on it and what ... scientist and morals. So they would inform you what a lot of Christians do believe. So in that respect like you know, inform you of that.

Interviewer: Right. But there was a clear distinction between the science and religion?

Jonathan: Yeah. In the science lesson religion didn't sway it. It wasn't—I mean, you do get some of these schools where you know, the controversial ones where you got, you know, they don't believe in evolution but they taught us evolution.

Interviewer: Right.

Jonathan: I mean, one day in an RE lesson I asked the teacher, you know, we know about evolution and we know about you know, how the world's billions of years old and something like that and how man's only been created recently. So, in the creation story, the seven-day story ... or whatever, I asked how does that stand in your views. The cop-out answer, well I thought it was cop-out was, 'day's a metaphor for time period'. So, they still believed it was God but a day wasn't, you know, a 24-hour period. It was like kind of a division.

Interviewer: But overall from what you've said to me, would it be all right the inference that this was a fairly sophisticated set-up? I mean, we're not dealing here with fundamentalism?

Jonathan: Not fundamentalism at all. It didn't ... As for fundamentalism, the parents wouldn't stand for it.

Interviewer: It seems fairly kind of liberal kind of place.

Jonathan: Yeah, they'd educate you and give you the options to choose. They'd still do the Communion but you'd get a choice, you know. If you wanted to say something, you could. So in that respect they didn't force you into anything. We had to go to Carol Service because it was a school activity, not particularly because it was a religious aspect but it was something that the whole school did. So, in that respect, you know, I didn't have to say prayers if I didn't want to. I could you know, a lot of people reciting a prayer, I could just sit and be quiet. In some schools you get told off if you don't join in. But they were fine with it, you know. Personal choice.

Interviewer: Last question. So do you think this kind of education is relevant for the twenty-first century?

Jonathan: I personally, yes. I don't believe in God but some people do and religion will live on. I'd rather people be educated in it properly. You could be educated—it's the personal choice of whether you want your children to be brought up with a Christian ethos. My Mum did and I've got the Christian ethos. I don't believe in all the Christian aspects but the ethos I've got. The Ten Commandments and everything like that, I understand and I believe in. Some hope! So, I'd say it has got a place. Everyone has to have a choice for themselves and for the children. So, there's no—I can't see any harm in keeping it, is probably the best way of putting it, you know. I wouldn't particularly go and set up extra church schools but there's no harm in it being there following the path of the education system.

Interviewer: Thank you for your time.

Jonathan: You're welcome.

Notes on contributor

Helen Johnson is Reader in Education, School of Education, Kingston University, UK.

Using reflective practice to explore the origins and consequences of cultural and faith perspectives

Helen Johnson

We shall not cease from exploration
And the end of all our exploring
Will be to arrive where we started
And to know the place for the first time.

T. S. Eliot, *Little Gidding*

Our context

It is a conventional view that contemporary British society has lost its memory of its past, left its traditions behind and become fragmented, sharing little if anything of a common perspective about its purpose and values. Influentially, the Polish British sociologist, Zygmunt Bauman (2003), talks of a liquid modern society where individuals have 'no bonds'. Nothing is given and accepted, the processes of self-definition and self-assertion are perpetual. Clearly much of Bauman's analysis rings true; but from a *personal* viewpoint it is possible to say that few, if any of us, leave the past behind by moving completely from one paradigm to another. Our personalities and identities, however transmuted, are based, in part, on previous experiences and interpretations that we take with us for some form of ontological security, as a reference point. The chapter by Robert Jones explores an unbroken commitment to a particular religious tradition that now expresses itself in a faith sector institution. Some relevant questions are perhaps why we make the choice of particular experiences over others; why they are significant: and why we integrate them into our sense of self, into the creation of our own identity.

Personal identity, as Lynne Scholefield's chapter about her journey of religious faith and culture shows, is a complicated concept that must be used with care. (It also reveals how private issues are sometimes found expressing themselves in the research projects chosen in our professional lives). Few, if any of us, have one convenient label that can be pinned upon us: we understand that we all have multiple and situational identities (Hall, 1996). Thus, teachers in schools and others working in a variety of educational institutional contexts do not have professional perspectives that can be confidently and totally based on 'taken-for-granted' unquestioned assumptions. Howard Worsley's account of opening a new faith school is full of *questioning* (as are Jonathan's answers in his interview). In this uncertainty, it is likely that the conceptualisation of the professional identity used, promoted and embodied by those involved in the educational process at its widest, will be based, at least, in part, in terms of how they have constructed the narratives around *their own*. Obviously enough, this construction of identity takes place in a wider societal context, which itself is not homogenous. It is in this context that attempts to find solutions to 'wicked' social problems are to be found. This 'wickedness' expresses the reality where there are competing definitions, for which contributory factors are hard to assess, and for which multi-policy frameworks and inter-agency collaboration are required. Education provides a context *par excellence* for 'wicked problems', since health, social work, schooling, welfare and policy interpenetrate where well-being and development of children and young people are concerned. It is this context that educational professionals—professors of education, chaplains, school governors, students—must manage and resolve into a course of action; but such a task and role highlights the tensions between professional autonomy and definition, government policy and compliance. Catherine Hill's reflection on children growing up in traumatic, chaotic contexts takes the discussion a long way from abstract discussions about rights. But of course, such rights are important, as are the interventions of priests, nuns and other humanitarian workers who are working from declared ethical positions, some religious, some secular. They are working in schools and outside to provide basic needs and to run psycho-social recovery programmes.

Restating the uncertainty of contemporary identity

Individual identity is drawn from many sources; one of the most public of these is perhaps culture. This is a self-evidently dense term, used by many disciplines, such as social anthropology, organisational behaviour and management studies, each with their own emphases and conceptualisations. Hofstede (2000) and others offer wide generalisations about societal culture that, if used carelessly, are perhaps as useful as birth signs in astrology. More dangerously they can be used to present social cultures in their 'national boxes' as homogeneous. However, the idea of a societal culture is a contextual convenience that pinpoints a locale with an examinable history, declared policies for the future and an educational system with identifiable operating processes and characteristics. Some societal cultures, especially those belonging to 'Old Europe', are now increasingly problematic and may be in the process of re-creating themselves. With such complexities and ongoing shifts in identity, it is clear that it is no simple task to explore and understand the full cultural hinterland that such identities or labels represent in compression. On a more specific level about changes in identity, it can be said that educational policies in schools around these areas attempt to reflect changes in the composition of British society.

Cultural diversity of various kinds—drawn from religion, ethnicity, language, subject disciplines and professional approaches—is also present in organisations. Hoyle (1986, p. 3) notes that: 'central to the concept (of culture) is the idea of value, that which is regarded as worthwhile by members of the group'. So, within any school and linked community it is likely, if not certain, that many subcultures will coexist. Each will reflect different 'worthwhiles' that may or may not correspond with the mainstream culture, that in Apple's terms (1996) holds hegemonic sway within the school or community or society as a whole. Such comments are seemingly self-evident but of great significance, as will be touched upon later, when samples are being constructed or interviewees selected. More mundanely, but with no less significance, will be the personal values of individuals that may be expressed overtly in political, social or religious allegiances or more subtly, as Goffman (1969) would have it, in the 'ordinariness' of everyday behaviour and interaction. All these (individual and collective) 'cultures' will interact in ways that are both predictable and unpredictable. These four reflections perhaps show the obvious: we all start from somewhere. These four very different individuals do however share a field and a professional location and function. Following C. Wright Mills (1970), in this way, reflective practice demonstrates how the private and public are linked. Such juxtaposition can easily be seen in the cases of the four educational professionals who have in their function the playing out as a role model for a variety of persons within their focal sets.

At a wider level, the multiplicity of roles, however categorised, and the interpretative nature of human experience has allowed 'soft' qualitative methods, under modernism rejected for its subjectivity and lack of numbers, to re-emerge as a useful means to collect data (Munro, 1998; Goodson & Sikes, 2001). It is the direct experience of the self, be it the private or public or some other, created and ordered by the interviewee (Ricoeur, 1974, 1980) that is addressed, not aggregated and presented in the researcher's predetermined categories and formats. The Canadian researchers, Clandinin and Connelly (1994, p. 415) state it simply: 'Experience ... is the stories people live. People live stories, and in the telling of them reaffirm them, and create new ones'. Given this, the particular importance of the life history in the professional development of teachers, head teachers and other educationalists is clear. For such development work to be meaningful and effective, it must be integrated into the individual's previous experience and learning. Thus, for this to happen the individual in all his/her complexity and uniqueness must be recognised and fully become part of the learning strategy. Standardisation and aggregation are met again in the 'one size fits all' approach to continuing professional development and hides the complexity of the post-modern world. For such interpretation of the larger historical scene to be meaningful, the individual's life history must be discovered and valued.

Notes on contributor

Helen Johnson is Reader in Education, School of Education, Kingston University, UK.

References

Apple, M. (1996) *Cultural politics and education* (Buckingham, Open University Press).
Bauman, Z. (2003) *Liquid love* (Cambridge, Polity).
Clandinin, D. & Connelly, F. (1994) Personal experience methods, in: N. Denzin & Y. Lincoln (Eds) *Handbook of qualitative research* (London, Sage), 413–427.
Goffman, E. (1969) *The presentation of self in everyday life* (Harmondsworth, Penguin).
Goodson, I. & Sikes, P. (2001) *Life history research in educational settings: learning from lives* (Buckingham, Open University Press).
Hall, S. (1996) 'Who needs identity?' in: P. DuGay, J. Evans & J. Redman (Eds) *Identity: a reader* (London, Sage).
Hofstede, G. (2000) *Culture's consequences* (Beverley Hills, CA, Sage).
Hoyle, E. (1986) *The politics of school management* (London, Hodder & Stoughton).
Mills Wright, C. (1970) *The sociological imagination* (Harmondsworth, Pelican).
Munro, P. (1998) *Subject to fiction: women teachers' life history narratives and the cultural politics of resistance* (Buckingham, Open University Press).
Ricoeur, P. (1974) *The conflict of interpretations* (Evanston, IL, Northwestern University Press).
Ricoeur, P. (1980) Narrative time, *Critical Enquiry,* 7(1), 160–180.

PART C: LESSONS FROM HISTORY AND THE INTERNATIONAL SCENE—AND GUESSES ABOUT THE FUTURE

Brief historical survey: the need to recognise old wine in new bottles—the structural roots of voluntarism and difference in the English schooling system

Marilyn Holness

The importance of structural forms within a system

The restructuring of the British public sector under Thatcherism has been much discussed (Pollitt, 1993) and can be seen as a watershed in the role of the state and the nature of the public services. The influence of these reforms is clear and persistent. For the current Labour government, first elected in 1997, is determined to continue the sector's reform by introducing new delivery mechanisms that respond to changing levels of expectations about service quality, and to wider, uncontrollable factors such as demographic trends. However, there is much in the public services that seemingly stays the same; and it is possible within the education service, in particular, to detect such a continuation of policy, structure and systems within policies that present themselves as new.

An example of such continuation and conservatism is the role played by the voluntary sector in current educational provision in England. The various voluntary bodies that comprise the booming voluntary sector in English state schooling are responsible for the church/faith schools that educate over a third of English children. The popularity of such schools with parents; their prominent role within governmental education policy; and the not infrequent openings of new faith schools have revived awareness of the importance of this sector.

This chapter will focus on the voluntary sector of schools as a systemic organisational issue. However, it must be noted that such a sector is not uniform, containing as it does many faith groups and many interpretations of their beliefs and values. Additionally, systemic concerns and general characteristics also express themselves in the operation of the individual school. A school, as with any organisation, will develop an infrastructure in order to achieve its aims and objectives. Such an infrastructure will be influenced by a school's own culture, purpose and mission, which, in the voluntary sector, will have both internal and external sources. It will also be influenced by contingencies, such as size, and importantly, in the public sector, through governmental intervention and intention. In order to operate successfully, the infrastructure will need to have the capacity to respond to and initiate change that emanates from both within and outside the sector and the individual school. Thus, in this way, it is clear that structural organisation and systemic design, in whatever form, cannot be regarded as a once-and-for-all exercise. Any change, however rationally planned, is likely to have some unpredictable results. But within this unpredictability, perhaps, it is also necessary to recognise how much things stay the same.

First, the chapter will offer a sketch of the history of the voluntary sector of schools as a systemic organisational involvement. This section will explore the origins of voluntarism and how it has survived as a presence and a structural influence in the otherwise much reformed English system. Then, with reference to the voluntary sector's current situation in England and the public debate now surrounding it, the chapter will go on to discuss on-going developments.

Change: a central governmental reluctance to intervene

The development of the public sector and its concomitants of social planning and large-scale public expenditure, as LeGrand (1982), amongst others, pointed out over twenty years ago, are very much phenomena of the twentieth century. The growth of government, both central and local, only accelerated with the emergence of the nation-state and capitalism. For, in England, it is not until the Industrial Revolution of the late eighteenth and early nineteenth century that the state felt it necessary to intervene in social matters. (Up to that time, the state had focused its concerns on the defence of the realm and the raising of the necessary taxes.)

This intervention was primarily to cope with the social consequences of industrialisation, the externalities produced by the free play of market forces. These resulted in harsh factory conditions, squalid housing, rampant epidemics and the other types of deprivation in the suddenly expanding cities. However, even as late as 1890, total government expenditure comprised less than 10% of the gross national product and nearly 50% of that was on defence (Peacock & Wiseman, 1961, quoted by LeGrand, 1982). However, central government had started to intervene in matters that hitherto had been regarded as the concern of the individual: health and education being two of the most notable examples. As will be seen, this intervention, particularly in the 1830s, took the form of providing grants from the public purse. This led to a growth in local ad hoc bodies as administrative and overall financial responsibility (and concomitant standardisation) were not initially accepted by central government. Then, as government gradually became more involved, some bodies were absorbed into the state and others remained independent and voluntary. Some of the policy-making actors and implementers became public servants; others did not, and some had and continue to hold an ambiguous position. Control, independence and ambiguity seem a curiously English mixture. It is this complexity that has implications for the dual system, its supporting bureaucracies such as local education authorities (LEAs) and voluntary bodies such as diocese education boards. This influence has been felt throughout the explosion of governmental intervention and control in the twentieth century—and today, at the beginning of the twenty-first century.

Change: the origins of today's dual and diversified schooling system

So, in the period in which central government was reluctant to provide elementary schooling, how did the children of the poor learn to read and write? Simply, prior to the nineteenth century, two-thirds of English children received no formal schooling. Individual philanthropists or private groups supplied the schools that existed for the poor. For as early as 1780, in response to the needs of children working in Gloucester's pin-making factories, businessman Robert Raikes had founded the Sunday School movement. In these popular schools, the teachers that taught reading and the catechism were voluntary workers.

   Whilst most voluntary schools, at this time, had religious underpinnings and purpose, the influence of secular philosophers, such as Rousseau, was also a feature of the late eighteenth and the early nineteenth centuries. This resulted in various experiments in schooling that were sympathetic to the educational and emotional needs of children. Pestalozzi (1746–1827) set up a progressive school in Switzerland. In England, the Infant School Movement, borrowing from both Rousseau and Pestalozzi, also established schools. But other developments were somewhat less child-centred. In the aforementioned Sunday schools and other day institutions such as the ragged schools for the poor, the monitorial principle, as developed in particular by Joseph Lancaster and Alexander Bell, was used. In its rigid method, use of older pupils as teachers and suitability for large class sizes, it produced economies of scale. In this way, the schools using such methods resembled the factories for which the children were destined.

From these individual efforts grew educational societies. Lancaster's Quaker and other nonconformist friends founded the Royal Lancasterian Society in 1808, which six years later was renamed the British and Foreign School Society (Pile, 1979). Its aims were delineated in its original title: 'The Institution for promoting the British system of education of the labouring and manufacturing classes of society of every religious persuasion'.

In 1811, the Anglicans set up the National Society for the Education of the Poor. The Church of England had long been involved in the education of children belonging to the social elite, both in terms of the two exclusive English universities of Oxford and Cambridge and 'public' schools. However, its participation in the education of the children of the less privileged and affluent as a declared strategy stretches back only into the nineteenth century. Involvement came about through its competition with the nonconformist churches, especially the Methodists, for the loyalties of the English working class. In the mid nineteenth century, the Roman Catholic Church strengthened its position as mass Irish emigration made a considerable impact in British cities and resulted in the opening of many new Catholic schools. Significantly, as the century progressed, Jewish refugees escaping from the pogroms of Eastern Europe also arrived and established their own schools, some with state funding. Hence the multicultural nature of the voluntary sector was established long before the term was even invented.

The 'other' part of the dual system

As has been seen, central government was reluctant to interfere with this voluntary activity of private charitable bodies, both religious and secular. So, when government felt compelled to make some form of gesture to indicate its concern, grants were made to assist the work of these two main bodies. In 1833, these societies received grants of a mere £10,000 each (Pile, 1979). As Sallis has remarked (1994, p. 8), it is clear that the current dual system of church/faith voluntary and state maintained schools had 'its origins in the grants made in 1833'. Such a dual system is unique among the sophisticated economies of the G7, and even among other countries that have direct cultural links with the United Kingdom. A secularist view of state schooling is the norm. The English system's voluntarist origins are also in marked contrast to other European nations. In France, Napoleon had founded a state schooling system in 1806, and this had had a profound influence on other nearby states: the Netherlands founded a state system of education in 1808 and Prussia introduced a state system of high schools (and universities) in 1810.

If the British government was initially reluctant to be involved in education, its role increased rapidly through the nineteenth century. Subsequent annual grants were increased, so by 1857 annual grants had risen to over £500,000 and to administer this sum, a Department of Education was set up. But as Pile (1979) tells us, it was not an ordinary department, created with a minister at the head of it. This was followed in 1870 by the Education Act, in response to internal political pressures as the trade unions agitated for compulsory education, in particular for the newly-enfranchised artisan class that had been granted the vote in 1867. Also important in any discussion of the massification of the English educational system was the Prussian example: as noted elsewhere, state education had existed from the very beginning of the nineteenth century, and its value in military matters had been demonstrated all over Europe. Additionally, employers were concerned about growing German and American competition and demanded elementary education for their workers as they saw that education meant increased efficiency.

The controversial dual system

Once state involvement had been established in schooling, the question had to be asked whether or not the voluntary sector should either be abolished or allowed to wither away. The controversial nature of the dual system has ebbed and flowed in public consciousness. When the Education Act 1902 incorporated Church of England and Roman Catholic schools into the state system, there were furious debates in the House of Commons. Balfour, then Prime Minister, had to defend the Act against opposition that demanded 'No Rome on the rates', and those arguments have a familiar ring today, albeit not necessarily focused on the same religious group. Such incorporation that provided for state funding for the Church of England and Catholic schools was, according to Balfour as he introduced the Bill in the House of Commons, *not* 'out of harmony with the needs of a progressive community'; for such schools 'part of the normal machinery for education' (Balfour, quoted in Munson, 1991, p. 245). However, such was the anger that was generated at this time that some 40 years later Churchill could warn Butler, as the epoch-making Education Act 1944 started on its progress through the committee stages of the House, to leave this hard-won settlement undisturbed (Barber, 1994). So 'sleeping dogs' were left to lie.

At the beginning of the twenty-first century, the dual system remains in operation and it can clearly be seen that the voluntary sector is not a historic relic in a long and terminal decline. The contrary is the case. Subsequent developments throughout the twentieth century have not only resulted in the survival of this voluntary sector of faith schools and their increasing popularity with parents in an otherwise rapidly secularising society; it is broadening out to include the schools of newly arrived immigrant groups (and has been seen to encourage the participation and partial funding by philanthropists in their modern-day guise as successful business people). Currently, this voluntary sector comprises these faith schools: Church of England; Roman Catholic; Methodist; Jewish; Muslim; Sikh; Greek Orthodox; Seventh Day Adventist. (Five of the Jewish schools and the Muslim, Sikh, Greek Orthodox and Seventh Day Adventist have moved into the state sector since 1997 (Woodward, 2001, p. 25).

The renewed debate about the continuing existence of the voluntary sector is recent; and, as noted earlier, such schools have been popular with parents in preference to schools in the maintained sector; their prominent role within governmental education policy has been greeted with both surprise and suspicion; and the expansion of the faith schools sector has clearly shown that it is not withering away. Additionally, although there is no empirical evidence to support this assertion, it could be that it has been provoked by the opening of Muslim state-funded schools and a general unease about the nature and consequences of Britain's multicultural society.

Structural foundations and developments

Developments in the post-Second World War period have been expressions of two very different approaches to the role of the state in education and the values underpinning the nature of state schooling. Under successive Labour governments since the 1960s until post-1997, the 'comprehensivisation' or uniformity of secondary schooling has been promoted to support the idea of the 'common school', managed by the democratically responsive LEA, in the spirit of egalitarianism. In marked contrast, the Conservatives' Education Act 1986 and Education Reform Act in 1988 produced the grant-maintained schools experiment. That policy, with echoes of the old direct grant grammar schools, was predicated on direct funding from central government to schools, intending to use the LEAs only as a conduit. Though subject to inspection by the central agency of Ofsted, such grant-maintained schools were essentially to operate as 'independent' institutions.

Thus, latterly, education, and schools in particular, have been subject to much change that expressed both these very different paradigms about the nature of the school: its management and supervision. Significantly, in all of this, the presence of the voluntary sector was not eliminated and remains an organisational and systemic reality. It is this reality that has become part of current Labour governmental policy and been extended in other organisational experiments such as the specialist schools. Schagen *et al.* (2002, p. ii; my italics) state:

> Both specialist and faith schools can be seen as part of the present government's drive to raise standards and promote *diversity*. The White Paper, *Schools Achieving Success,* published in 2001, announced plans for new specialisms and a large increase in the number of specialist schools: it also advocated an expansion in the number of faith schools.

These historic origins and subsequent legislation have produced a structurally *varied* schooling system that contains schools that can be categorised in many ways, for example:

- maintained schools, which may be community, voluntary-aided, voluntary controlled or foundation schools
- grammar schools
- partially selective schools
- mixed or single-sex schools
- beacon schools
- specialist colleges
- city technology colleges
- city academies

The city academies' initiative is the most recent innovation where the English schooling system's deep roots in voluntarism can be identified. In May 2000, the Standards

Unit (of the then DfEE) declared that the sponsors of the new schools, with up to 20% of private and voluntary sponsorship, could be: 'businesses, individuals, churches and other faith groups, voluntary bodies, or partnerships within or across these categories'.

Thus, far from being eliminated, the presence of voluntarism has been broadened and in so doing has returned to the mixture of both secular and religious sources of the eighteenth and nineteenth century. This broadening out now includes the sponsorship of these academies by bodies such as the Christian educational charity, Church Schools Company, and other schools, including private ones. For example, in May 2004, Dulwich College 'joined a growing band of private schools forming links with state schools' (*TES*, 28 May 2004, p. 3). Seemingly little that is *completely* new in terms of structural forms has been introduced and much recycling has been done whatever the political complexion of the government in power at any particular time.

In conclusion: the past is prologue

In the face of the political and social realities of the twenty-first century as they start to roll out, what can be said about voluntary faith schools and their role in the education of English children in a world where religious difference has taken on a new significance?

As was seen earlier, it was necessary for Balfour to argue at the very beginning of the twentieth century that church schools were not inappropriate to the needs and objectives of a 'progressive community'. They were to be seen then as part of 'the normal machinery of education' in England (Barber, 1994, p. 41). Five years ago, it was possible to say that opposition to such schools was not an organised and substantial challenge (Johnson, 2000), either from academic and political sources.

Then, the liberal case in its form as a 'universal regime' was being made in two main ways in the public arena: first through the campaigns of journalists. The academic case was made in part, at least, through a discourse of silence that ignored the existence of the voluntary sector and the particular nature of its contribution.

It once appeared that secularisation and a 'sleeping' toleration, perhaps based on a hegemonic discourse of the 'universal regime', would allow faith schools to survive, without much media and academic attention. Global events, demographic trends, migration, cultural developments, and governmental education policy that perhaps—recognising the realities of the new world order—wants these schools not merely to survive but thrive, have challenged that toleration in its prevailing form. A new century and a new world are perhaps demanding a toleration that enable, as Gray says (2000, p. 1), human beings and their schools 'to flourish in many ways of life'; and that too, is part of the liberal tradition. What is clear is that the organisational 'hotch potch' of the first part of the nineteenth century and earlier gave way to the dual system that under LEA control became increasingly 'standardised' but was never uniform. Then, under the DfES (and its predecessors) the system became 'centralised' while managerial responsibility was devolved to individual schools. The system remains controlled but fragmented as might be expected in a postmodern world. Such fragmentation or variety has, as has been seen, always been there from the very birth of the system. Thus, the growth of specialisation and other expressions of diversity in England can be seen as an incremental *organisational and systemic* development based on historical and operational precedence. That is the gift of the voluntary sector.

Notes on contributor

Marilyn Holness is the Deputy Principal of Southlands College, Roehampton University, UK.

References

Barber, M. (1994) *The making of the 1944 Education Act* (London, Cassell).

Gray, J. (2000) *Two faces of liberalism* (Cambridge, Polity).

Johnson, H. (2000) Surviving and thriving in a secularized culture: the phenomenon of religious (church/faith) schools in England, *The Journal of Research on Christian Education*, 9(1), 115–135.

Legrand, J. (1982) *The strategy of equality* (London, Allen & Unwin).

Munson, J. (1991) *The Nonconformists: in search of a lost culture* (London, SPCK).

Pile, W. (1979) *The Department of Education and Science* (London, Allen & Unwin).

Pollitt, C. (1993) *Managerialism and the public services* (2nd edn) (Oxford, Blackwell).

Sallis, J. (1994) *Free for all?* (London, CASE).

Schagen, S., Davies, D., Rudd, P. & Schagen, I. (2002) *The impact of specialist and faith schools on performance* (Slough, NFER).

Woodward, W. (2001, December 12) Faith in the system, *The Guardian*, p. 25.

The dialectic of Australian Catholic education

Denis McLaughlin

Introduction

Catholic education in Australia is a popular commodity, not only with Catholics who make up 27% of the population, but increasingly with Australians of other faiths and none. Catholicism is the largest single denomination in Australia (Hughes, 2000). There are approximately 1700 Catholic schools, in which 57,000 teachers educate 665,000 students. This is approximately 20% of Australia's school-age population. Thirty percent of Australians choose to send their children to non-government schools, with Catholic education being Australia's largest non-government employer. Such decisions by parents involve considerable financial outlays, for while federal and state governments substantially support private schools with funds, parents annually contribute school fees of many thousands of dollars, a phenomenon that prevents many Catholic parents sending their children to Catholic schools (Chesterton & Johnston, 1998; Catholic Education Commission of Victoria, 2004).

The Australian Catholic Church is officially energetically committed to its school networks consisting of systemic schools, ultimately under the responsibility of a diocesan bishop, and Independent Catholic schools controlled by the executive of one of the many Religious Institutes (National Catholic Education Commission, 2000). Despite this commitment, there are some reservations concerning the authenticity of Catholic schools coming from some clergy:

> The (secondary) schools were seen by 46% of the priests as burdens on parish resources with little return for the local community. 'A low level of religious practice among students, parents and teachers' (56%) and the perception that 'the overall agenda of the schools has little to do with partnership with the local parish' were some of the reasons offered by members of the clergy for their negative attitudes towards Catholic secondary schools. (Tinsey, 1998, p. 67)

The basis of these reservations is the differing expectations stakeholders in Catholic education have concerning the purpose of Catholic education. Until recently, there had been relative unanimity about the purpose of Australian Catholic education (Praetz, 1980). This is no longer the case. This chapter will explore the new pluralism of Australian Catholic education and discuss some of the implications for this new reality. In particular, the argument underpinning this chapter is that stakeholders in Australian Catholic education often hold beliefs inconsistent with official Catholic teaching as documented in the *Catechism of the Catholic Church*. The chapter will conclude by offering three realistic purposes for Catholic education which are relevant and consistent with pluralistic views held by stakeholders.

Such a pluralism was absent at the formal beginnings of Australian Catholic education in the 1880s when Australia's Catholic bishops made their decision to establish a separate Catholic school system in defiance of the free, secular and compulsory schools that the various colonial governments began to provide. Catholic education was seen to fulfil at least three purposes then (Fogarty, 1959).

Original purposes of Catholic education

The first one is very adequately summarised by Irish Christian Brother, Bernard O'Hagan at the opening of the Brothers' first Sydney school in 1887: 'Our main object shall ever to be to value above all things their eternal salvation, and to secure this by faithfully and steadfastly adhering to the faith of their fathers' (Greening, 1989).

The second purpose implicit in the later part of O'Hagan's speech was to reproduce a religious culture, as exemplified by the words of Archbishop Vaughan (cited by Fogarty, 1957, p. v): 'Dearest people, bring up your children thorough Catholics. Steep them during childhood and youth if possible, deep in the Catholic faith. Make them conscious of the burden they will have to bear'. Such a culture amplified and extended a Catholic world view to counteract Protestantism and even worse still, the fun-loving secularism characteristic of Australians (Mackay, 1999, p. 231).

The third reason for the establishment of an alternative Catholic school system revolved around the tribal Irishness of the Catholic population. This tribalism became the conduit to combine two sets of contradictory objectives. Both have their roots in the origins of the people. The Irish saw themselves not only as a group which was socially disadvantaged, but as an outpost of Erin, which had endured centuries of English cruelty (Campion, 1982). This institutionalized oppression continued against them in colonial Australia. As in Ireland, so in Australia, the Church became the focus of Irish identity and culture and the strongest political vehicle to gain and bargain for social gains. Indeed, Irishness and Catholicism became tautological concepts in colonial Australia. Consequently, the Catholic school was seen as: 'a refuge which the Catholic Church had created for itself as a protection against what was sometimes seen as a hostile environment. Paradoxically, however, Catholics came to see their schools as means for their children to belong to and succeed in the wider society' (Turner, 1992, p.171), a society that was hostile to Irish Catholicism. For the Irish Catholic, education was the only practical vehicle available to them to redress their injustices through 'upward social mobility' (Turner, 1992, p. 171) into the very society from which the Catholic school was supposed to shield their young. The sad irony of this purpose of Catholic education was that many Catholics did, in fact, gain entry into the Anglo-Protestant establishment, wanting more to join that hegemonic group and to enjoys its fruits, than to change and challenge it (Ryan & McLaughlin, 1999).

These aims were more or less honoured in Catholic schools up until the 1950s and 1960s, but they seem irrelevant in the twenty-first century. Talk of gaining or losing eternal salvation has negligible interest among modern Australian youth (Tacey, 2002). Moreover, an identifiable Catholic culture has largely evaporated, and for the most part has been absorbed into mainstream Australia. Given this reality, Australian bishops feel they must have defensible answers to Roman Curia Officials about the reasons for the freefall of the number of Catholics who regularly attend the sacraments (McGillion, 2003). Currently, only 13.3% of Australian Catholics attend Mass weekly (Dixon, 2003). This trend downwards looks likely to continue.

On a more positive note, it is undeniable that Australian Catholic schools have been outstandingly successful in promoting upward social mobility, particularly over the past 50 years. Catholics had gained complete access into the so-called Protestant establishment, when in 1996 Irish Catholics Paul Keating became Prime Minister, Sir William Deane was Governor General and Sir Gerard Brennan Chief Justice of the High Court. Indeed, to the chagrin of the Australian Labor Party, the traditional party of Catholics, that bastion of White Anglo-Saxon Protestantism, the Liberal Party has been accused of being 'Catholicized'. Without a doubt Catholic education has been a significant contributor to this mobility, not so much by addressing the injustices in our society, but by, in so many ways, accepting the agenda of the Protestant establishment by becoming part of it, and indeed attaining leadership roles within it (Ryan and McLaughlin, 1999). Such a gain for Catholic education is a Pyrrhic victory when compared with the integrity of values proposed in the gospel.

Given such a context, it is not surprising that the bishops have commissioned research to better articulate the nature and purpose of Catholic schooling in Australia (McLaughlin, 2000; Queensland Catholic Education Commission, 2001). Both these projects generated a catalogue of defining features, but their authenticity has to be critiqued against their usefulness in real circumstances. Espoused directions need to be critiqued. They may have answered yesterday's questions, albeit inadequately, but the question which demands exploration is: 'do they address contemporary realities no matter how unsavory these are?' Some analysis of the realities about contemporary Australian Catholic education is needed. This will be attempted by listening to the voices of three major stakeholders in Catholic education: parents; students and teachers.

The parents

It is true that parents are enthusiastic supporters of Catholic education. but which parents are the supporters? Slightly less than 50% of Catholic children attend Catholic schools. It is the poorer children, and increasingly, richer children who are not attending Catholic schools (Griffiths, 1999). For the poor, school fees have been identified as the main deterrent for these Catholic children not attending Catholic schools. Moreover, in the most deprived population of Catholic Australians, Aboriginal children are proportionally under-represented in Catholic schools because their parents do not want charity to meet the fees of Catholic schools (Chesterton & Johnston, 1998). Ironically, it is the middle-class non-Catholics, dissatisfied with a government education, who want the academic values and discipline that Catholic schools offer, and it is this strata of the population who can now afford to send their children to Catholic schools. In some Catholic secondary schools, over 40% of the population is non-Catholic. Their presence makes the school viable. Moreover, most Catholic parents who send their children to Catholic schools do not regularly practise Catholicism, as Figure 1 (from Dixon, 2003) indicates.

The point to conclude is that the vast majority of parents who are sending children to Catholic schools either do not practise Catholicism or are not Catholics. In

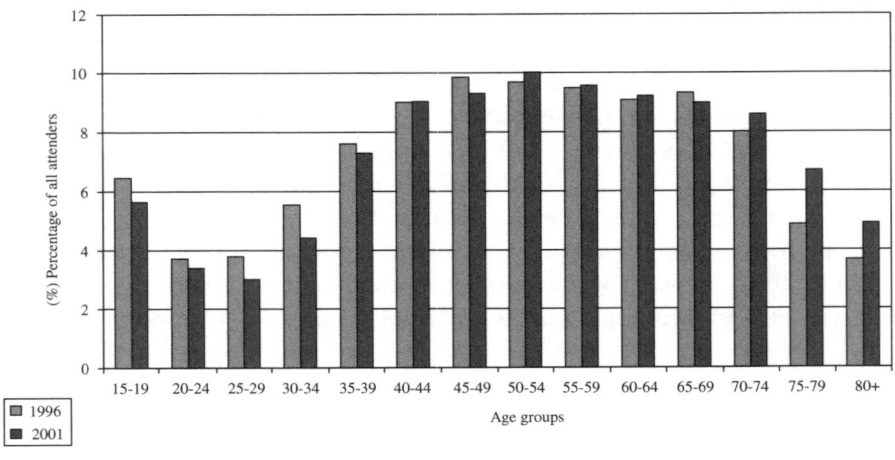

Figure 1.   Age profile of Mass attenders (1996 and 2001)

addition there is a considerable plurality of views among Catholics who do practise. Table 1 (from Dixon, 2004) provides information of beliefs from approximately 9000 *practising* Catholics. Such data offer challenges to those who lead and teach in Catholic schools. Certainly the purpose of Catholic education invites rethinking, as does the content of religious education syllabuses, if what is taught is to have any relevant impact. Moreover, Sultmann, Thurgood and Rasmussen (2003), in an extensive survey involving parents who chose to send or not send their children to Catholic schools, concluded that quality of teaching, care of children and school discipline were the main reasons why they sent their children to Catholic schools. Catholicism as a religion was number 14 on their list.

A conclusion to be drawn from such data is that the vast majority who send their children to Catholic schools are seeking the education standards (Arthur, 2002) and human values experienced in Catholic schools, but are not committing themselves to formal Catholicism as their religion of practice. This means for some that Catholic schools have failed to hand on a 'holistic' Catholic culture and to all intended purposes offer an education 'practically indistinguishable' from government schools (Arthur, 1995, p. 253). For others, it becomes a challenge to nurture a more open Catholicism, reassessing educational goals in the light of kingdom imperatives (Edmund Rice Education, Australia, 2004).

One of the problems with this changing demographic is that, at least in some places, this changing parent population wants the Catholic school to welcome a grammar elitist school culture. The point to note is that the financial tail could well wag the Catholic dog up the semi-elitist path. Elitism and Catholic education is a supposed oxymoron (Congregation for Catholic Education, 1998, p. 16). It also seems that Australian education is following an American trend, that the more wealthy Catholics are sending their children to the endowed non-Catholic private schools. Though statistics are difficult to come by under Australian privacy legislation, anecdotal information suggests that approximately 30% of students in the more elite and richer independent and Protestant schools are Catholic.

There is current debate about this new phenomenon in Australian Catholic education. Some have called for an increase in the number of 'rich' Catholic schools, which can provide more for the growing proportion of wealthy Catholic parents, who will continue to send their children to the elite private schools which in many ways clearly can offer more. It is simplistic to dismiss this issue as one of snobbery, for one of the best things caring parents can do for their children is to provide them with the best education they can afford. If this cannot be provided in a Catholic school, parents choose others that more adequately meet their expectations. So the dilemma is, if fees are increased to provide more resources in Catholic schools, an increased proportion of poorer Catholics leave the system. If fees are not increased, more wealthy children leave Catholic schools and their places are taken by middle-class non-Catholics. The dilemma is more than a financial one, it is about authenticity. The failure to explore this may well foster the dialectic of maintaining Catholic schools and systems operating as ends in themselves, 'for the good of the College', rather than as a means to serve. Australian Catholic education then adopts the class divisions operating in many

Table 1.   Responses by generation to items about Church doctrine and moral teachings. These sample populations are practising Catholics

Church doctrine or moral teaching	Pre-Boomers (%)	Baby Boomers 47–59 (%)	Gen X 25–46 (%)	Post-school Gen Y (18–24) (%)
Virginity of Mary				
Mary conceived Jesus w/out intercourse	81	74	76	73
Mary's virginity is not to be taken literally	19	26	25	27
Number of respondents (N) = 8890				
Eucharist: the bread and wine …				
… truly become Body & Blood of Christ	81	69	61	53
… remain bread and wine	19	31	40	47
N = 7737				
Understanding of God				
One God, Father, Son & Holy Spirit	78	71	71	61
God exists, but not as Trinity	21	29	28	36
We cannot know if God exists	1	1	1	3
God does not exist	0	0	0	0
N = 9607				
Abortion				
Always morally wrong	64	50	43	34
Justified only in extreme circumstances	31	39	42	47
Justified widely but not always	5	10	14	18
Never wrong	0	1	1	1
N = 9412				
Premarital sex				
Always morally wrong	65	41	35	27
Not wrong if in a committed relationship	33	52	55	58
Never wrong	2	6	10	16
N = 9251				

Note: All results significant at p < .001 level.
Source: *2001 National Church Life Survey* in Dixon (2004).

Table 2.   Motivations parents have for sending their children to school (Sultmann *et al.*, 2003)

Criteria	Government	Independent	Catholic
Care of students	100%	92%	90%
Quality teaching/education	92%	94%	94%
School discipline	88%	85%	90%
Consultation with parents	100%	76%	68%
Moral development	68%	80%	84%
Vision/Principles/Values	75%	73%	78%

private school systems. Instead of being counter-cultural, alternative or creative, the Catholic school system replicates the status quo and clones government school systems and then says it is somehow different. Clearly, some parents want class divisions, but those who are responsible for Catholic education have to consider if parents are the final arbiters of authenticity.

The students

The second stakeholder of contemporary Australian Catholic education is students. Given the results from the analysis of parents sending their children to Catholic schools undertaken in the previous section, it is not unexpected that comparatively few Catholic children practise their faith. Table 3 (from Dixon, 2003), generated from census statistics, provides evidence for this assertion.

Likewise there is a dramatic fall off in practice once Catholics school students leave school.

> At the Australian Catholic University in Sydney, a report has indicated that up to 97% of young Catholics abandon the practice of their faith within twelve months of completing high school. In Melbourne, the late B.A. Santamaria found this figure so astonishing that he set about to conduct a similar survey in his own metropolitan area. Santamaria's report confirmed that approximately 94% of graduates from Catholic secondary schools had defected from established faith practices within twelve months of completing their education. (Tacey, 2000, p. 190)

There are two Australian research projects that have relatively large samples of school-age Catholics indicating their beliefs and values. One is Flynn and Mok's (2002) which had a sample of 8310 Grade 12 students, and the other is the Australian

Table 3.   Mass-going Australian children aged from 0–19

Age group	2001		
	Attenders (aged 15 and over) (%)	All attenders (%)	Attenders (to nearest thousand)
0–14	n/a	16.6	127,000
15–19	5.6	4.7	36,000

Table 4.   Responses by generation to items about Church doctrine and moral teachings. These
sample populations are practising Catholics

Church doctrine or moral teaching	School age (15–17) (%)
Number of respondents (N) = 346)	
Virginity of Mary	
Mary conceived Jesus w/out intercourse	74
Mary's virginity is not to be taken literally	26
Eucharist: the bread and wine …	
… truly become Body & Blood of Christ	46
… remain bread and wine	55
Understanding of God	
One God, Father, Son & Holy Spirit	51
God exists, but not as Trinity	43
We cannot know if God exists	5
God does not exist	1
Abortion	
Always morally wrong	31
Justified only in extreme circumstances	45
Justified widely but not always	19
Never wrong	4
Premarital sex	
Always morally wrong	20
Not wrong if in a committed relationship	56
Never wrong	24

Note: All results significant at $p < .001$ level.
Source: 2001 National Church Life Survey in Dixon (2004).

Bishops' National Life Survey of 346 practising Catholic students (Dixon, 2003,
2004). Both offer insights into what Australian school-age Catholics believe and
value. Some issues identified in the research will be discussed.

Idea of God

Though most students in Catholic schools acknowledge a belief in God, most were
unclear about the meaning of God, even among practising Catholics, where just on
half expressed the Trinity as the dominant image. David Tacey (2002) asserts that
the most dominant image of God among young Australians undertaking his
'Introduction to Spirituality' course at Melbourne University, was theistic. From
such a perspective God is understood as the omnipotent being very similar to the all
powerful, omniscient super deity, Zeus of Greek mythology. 'Theism' refers to belief
in one almighty God, who is creator and guide of the universe. Perhaps the concept
of an omniscient puppeteer or a divine Santa Claus, who records who has been
naughty and nice and gives presents to the nice would be closer to the mark. Such an

Table 5. Students' religious commitment and values 1998 (Flynn & Mok, 2002, p. 251)

Students' Religious Commitments and values	% agree	% disagree
I believe in God	86	8
God is a loving father who loves me very much	73	11
Christ is a real person to me in my daily life	69	9
I believe God always forgives me	69	9
I have experienced times when I felt close to God	55	21
Knowing Jesus helps me to be a better person	51	21
Jesus Christ is truly God	51	15
Jesus Christ is truly present in the Eucharist	51	13
I try to spend some time in prayer each day	40	42
I try to base my life on the teaching and example of Jesus	37	28
Religion helps me to answer questions about life	34	57
Jesus Christ is truly man	33	18
Average response	54.1	21.0

image is common enough in fundamentalist Christianity but will not sustain reflective and educated people. Theism is a distortion of the nature of God. Tacey asserts that this view of God and its accompanying dualism is the dominant image young people have of God when they leave Australian schools.

Jesus' influence on young people's lives

Most Catholic students responded overwhelmingly that Jesus had some influence on their lives. What is alarming is not the 51% who believe in the divine nature of Jesus but the low 33% who accepted the humanity of Jesus (33%). Jesus is perceived as another Superman or Batman or Spiderman or Dr Spock or moral policeman (Hughes, 2002). The essential core of Christianity, the incarnation, appears practically to have evaporated in the lives of Catholic youth. The mystery of Christ has been distorted by images of a magic Jesus, who once regularly intervened into laws of humanity through miracles and healings. When Jesus apparently fails to hear the pleading prayers of the contemporary young, both the magic Jesus and the mystery of Christ is jettisoned. Sadly, too many Catholic schools have failed to nurture the mystery, for it to be embraced or rejected. Catholic educators have to ask themselves if the Jesus taught to students in Catholic schools is the interventionist magician generated from a fundamentalist understanding of the gospels (Holloway, 2002, p. 60). Does the rational and critical rigour acquired by students in their Catholic schools ironically contribute to students rejecting a distorted image of Jesus received in religion classes? The ultimate challenge for the contemporary Catholic school is to provide an environment where the incarnated Christ experience introduces students to the dialectic that all humans are at their fundamental essence spiritual beings having a human experience not the converse (de Chardin, in Bowell, 2004, p. vii).

As a result, the dominant spirituality of many of the young is creation-focused and devoid of the Christ mystery. The youth see their world, though imperfect, as positive, and the vast majority of people they meet as good. The world is capable of being developed and they are optimistic about their ability to make the best of their lives and indeed improve the world. They believe they will do a better job than their parents. Consequently, they do not see that active membership of the institutional Church or the Jesus learnt at school as all that important or relevant. To put it bluntly, the world in which young Australians live is so alien from the world of churchmen as to make formal religion appear irrelevant for them (Mullins, 2003). That is not to say that the youth are not seeking a spiritual dimension to their lives. They are just not finding the institutional Churches as nurturers of a spirituality that seems relevant to their living. David Tacey's observation accurately reflects the reality of Australian young Catholics and their Church:

> In the past youth did not protest too much when they failed to understand religious language, because the Church held some fearsome moral authority over their lives and youth were threatened with punishment and eternal damnation if they did not submit to Church authority. But today's youth are more experimental, with more trust with the integrity of their own experience, so that the old threats of hellfire no longer create guilty conformity to Church expectations. (Tacey, 2000, p. 196)

Eucharist

For Catholics, the Eucharist is described as the source and summit of their religion (*Dogmatic constitution on the Church*, 1964, p. 11). Yet data from both research sources indicate that students have a lack of clarity about the meaning of Eucharist. Describing Eucharist in terms of the body and blood of Christ may contribute to this opaqueness. In terms of lived experience, one's understanding of body is restricted to immediate experience. Eucharist has as its focus in faith on the resurrected not resuscitated Christ (O'Loughlin, 2000) and the imagery of the body and blood of a pre-Easter Jesus, particularly when this is linked to the Last Supper, may contribute to the confusion. If Eucharist is primarily about the continued real presence of the glorified Christ through faith, why not use language such as 'real presence' instead of 'body and blood'? Certainly, the resurrected Christ does not possess a body in the same way a human possesses a body. Once again, the mystery of the Christ's presence may be suffocated by some apparent magical perception of Catholics supposedly eating a pre-Easter Christ's human flesh. A catechesis that authentically teaches this central tenet of Catholic faith to a youth demanding something more than more of the same, has yet to be developed.

Abortion

For the general public, the Church's teaching on abortion has been uncompromising and clear—more so, perhaps, than in any other area. Indeed, often in society and especially in Catholic circles, 'abortion has become such a highly charged emotional question, that a calm rational treatment is extremely difficult' (Eagan, 1995, p. 303). So it is surprising that only 20% of the practising Catholic students accepted unconditionally the Church's teaching on abortion, with 45% believing it to be justified in extreme circumstances, and 19% believing it to be permissible for a wider range of circumstances. These data are not exceptional, in that they do reflect a growing trend identified in other research of Catholic students. Flynn (1993, p. 312) reported that only 35% of Grade 12 students believed abortion to be a worse evil than the birth of an unwanted child, while 58% believed it permissible if the pregnancy was a result of rape. While this topic was surveyed in their later research, Flynn and Mok (2002) chose not to report their results. There is a consistent trend in the research reported in this paper from parents, students and teachers, for all three groups to have a more flexible view on this topic than that articulated in official Catholic teaching. What is surprising is that flexibility is observed among both practising and non-practising Catholics.

Implications

One might reflect on the reasons for this current state of affairs among students in Roman Catholic schools. Until more research is done this may be only conjecture. Paul VI (1982,) was particularly insightful when he asserted: 'The split between the Gospel and culture is without doubt the drama of our time'. Cardinal Ratzinger believes that part of the reason for this secularization is that cultures like Australia have a 'liberal-radical ideology of an individualistic, rationalistic and hedonistic stamp' (Allen, 2000), a perspective diametrically contrary to the Gospel. This conclusion appears to the author too simplistic. While not ignoring the crass selfishness of some youth, there is also a wonderful generosity in Australian youth as shown by their response to the recent tsunami appeals. For many the authentic Gospel is seen as being distorted by 2000 years of white, European, male cultural accretions of institutional Roman Catholic traditions. Tom Kenneally, Australia's quintessential Catholic author, articulated his problem with Catholicism in the following words, which seem to resonate with an increasing number of Australian Catholics: 'The crisis (of faith) came from my realization that, behind the compelling mystery of Catholicism ... lay a cold and largely self interested corporate institution' (Charlton, 2002, p. 13). If leaders in Catholic education are to reconnect a largely alienated Catholic youth to the Church, then the challenge for this leadership is to live the mystery of Christ and bury the corporation of an over-institutionalized Church. Nothing less is good enough; nothing else is as compelling. Now is the time for selfless service and meaningful deeds, a point not lost on a twentieth-century pontiff:

> As we said recently to a group of lay people. 'Modern man (sic) listens more willingly to witnesses than to teachers, and if he does listen to teachers, it is because they are witnesses' ... It is therefore primarily by her conduct and by her life that the Church will evangelise the world: (Paul VI, 1975)

The teachers

The third stakeholder of contemporary Australian Catholic education is teachers. There is little hard data on what Australian Catholic teachers believe and value. In order to begin to address this lacuna in the research, McLaughlin, Begg, Pollard and Wilkinson (2005) researched 228 teachers from three middle-class urban high schools.[1] Here we report on some of the results.

The undisputed conclusion to make is that the vast majority of Catholic teachers in this sample have reservations about the contemporary Catholic Church, their employer (Table 6). Most, like the general Catholic population, are not regularly practising. What is of interest is that this research confirms the conclusions of other studies

Table 6. Some results concerning faith beliefs and practices of teachers in Australian Catholic schools

Church doctrine or moral teaching	
Number of respondents (N) = 228	Teachers in catholic schools (%)
Virginity of Mary	
Mary conceived Jesus w/out intercourse	23.80
Mary's virginity is not to be taken literally	52.40
Eucharist: the bread and wine ...	
Truly become Body & Blood of Christ	34.20
Remain bread and wine	1.00
Makes present Christ's sacrifice	14.90
Symbolizes Christ sacrifice	23.80
Understanding of God	
One God, Father, Son & Holy Spirit	45.00
God exists, but not as Trinity	1.00
We and Universe are one	31.20
Mass attendance...	
Rarely or special occasions	27.70
Less than monthly	17.80
Once a month	12.40
2 or 3 times a month	9.40
Weekly or more	31.70
Divorce	
Always morally wrong	0.50
Not wrong in extreme circumstances	16.80
Not wrong in wider range of circumstances	21.80
Personal matter for couple	58.90
Contraception	
Always morally wrong	1.00
Not wrong in extreme circumstances	3.50
Justified in many circumstances but not in every case	12.90
Personal matter for couple	58.90

that identify that practising Catholics are no less likely than non-practising Catholics to decide personally on what they choose to believe. The following quotation is a fairly accurate description to explain the behaviour of Australian Catholic teachers:

> If they agree with the Church on an issue, it is because the Church position makes sense to them and they actively decide to agree. If a Church teaching does not make sense to them, they will refuse to agree, no matter how often or how clearly or how authoritatively the church has spoken on it. (Gremillion and Castelli, 1988)

There seems to be a sort of parallel Church operating now in Australia. Both sectors of the Church have in them laypeople, priests and religious. One is the institutional Catholic Church, with a focus on the organization, the curia, the Magisterium. The other sees the Church more in terms of the 'People of God' and views the institution as more and more out of touch with their reality, focusing too much on law, power and authority and too little on service, justice and compassion.

The research indicates that this latter group is not composed of young revolutionaries and noisy dissidents. They are ordinary mums and dads, whose own parents were probably practising traditional Catholics. Like their parents, they are very much at home with the Catholic tradition, but unlike their parents they ignore many of the rules that institutional Catholicism legislates as important. The ultimate reasons for this change of behaviour are values and leadership credibility. The unwavering obedience Catholics gave to their Church has now become conditional. The Church's credibility in many areas has become suspect, not only because of the child abuse scandal but also because of the inauthentic responses to this issue from many in leadership positions (Ormerod and Ormerod, 1995; Cozzens, 2000). For the Australian Catholic teacher, it is ultimately the family that provides meaning and it is the family that generates energy. What priests and prelates want and say does not attract similar meaning or energy. Much of what Catholics criticize in the Church is the lack of relevance between what the Church thinks important and the lived experience of ordinary Catholics. Teachers do not want to get involved in polemics and debates. As employees of the institutional Church, they keep silent in order to save their jobs, pay their mortgages, scrimp for their children's school fees and contribute to their superannuation. Hassles with the official Church is the last thing they want. Probably this tenuous relationship of Catholic teachers with their employer is aptly illustrated with this quotation from an assignment mailed for correction:

> I define myself as a professional Catholic, not in a derogatory sense but as a statement of fact. The Catholic Church employs me; my future career depends to a large extent on my relationship with the Parish Priest and my involvement with the local Parish—especially liturgically. I therefore regularly read to the assembled community and teach students Church teachings such as the Assumption—something I do not believe happened. It is my role to teach the children the accumulated knowledge and tradition of the Catholic Church, what Morwood calls the conventional stage of faith. Morwood describes this conventional stage as both good and a necessary stage. This may be true. However as educators would we knowingly teach a Mathematics concept which we know could not possibly be true? Yet, the school liturgy to celebrate the Assumption is prepared and will be a compulsory activity for all children and last week's newsletter contained a reflection based on the Assumption. Questions such as 'How true am I being to my own spirituality?' and 'Am I

treating the Catholic Church justly by not being totally committed to and adhering to its teachings?' began to nag me. True, with selected trusted friends and colleagues such questions as 'who is Jesus?' are discussed openly (usually at night); but should I continue to play this charade? Disturbing thoughts when you have a mortgage and children to educate!

One of the questionnaire items asked respondents to list certain behaviours in terms of wrong doing (O'Donnell, 2001). Table 7 shows a tabulated set of results ranking wrong-doing in terms of seriousness. The most serious is first. Though the ratings indicate that respondents find many of the behaviours very serious, the mean aggregates illustrate clearly that wrongness in the family holds a greater degree of seriousness. Australian Catholic teachers in the main appear to be getting on with their lives and make many personal decisions based not so much on the benchmarks of Church teachings but on the benchmarks of personal experience and their own family values.

Another phenomenon the author has noted in the last five tears as guest speaker to about fifty gatherings of teachers in all the mainland Australian states, New Zealand, Mauritius, South Africa and Papua New Guinea, is that the majority of teachers volunteer that they do not believe in original sin. One of the questionnaire items (Table 8) sought clarification from the statement: 'All humans are born with original sin on their souls'.

The following discussion is speculative, gathered from anecdotal data from meetings of hundreds of teachers at these venues. They need to be tested by more comprehensive research. The reason why this teaching is repudiated is the repugnant image that is painted of God the Father. This is a God who would require human sacrifice of his own son in order to reconcile his own creation to himself. In the era of child abuse, this image of God is particularly odious. Likewise, the story of Original Sin's introduction into human history as portrayed by the Catechism of the Catholic Church (CCC) is embarrassingly facile, contradictory and literalist: 'The account of the fall in Genesis 3 uses figurative language, but affirms a primeval event, a deed that

Table 7.   Wrong-doing behaviours ranged in order of seriousness

Wrong-doing	Mean rating out of 5
Child sex abuse	4.9912
Physical abuse in marriage	4.9430
Lack of concern about human rights of others	4.5482
Ruining a person's good	4.4430
Drug abuse	4.3596
Living a life of hypocrisy	4.2544
Alcohol abuse	4.2149
Stealing $500.00 or property worth $500.00	4.1404
Greediness; ignoring others' needs	4.0789
Damaging the environment	3.9561
Euthanasia	3.3728
Casual sex	3.3509
Smoking marijuana	3.0395

Table 8.   Teachers' beliefs in the Church teaching on Original Sin

I agree	I probably agree	I am uncertain	I disagree	I emphatically disagree
14.4%	8.9	13.9	23.3	38.1

took place at the beginning of the history of man' (CCC # 390). It also asserts that this dogma is central to Catholicism's theological framework and cannot be modified: 'The Church, which has the mind of Christ, knows very well that we cannot tamper with the revelation of original sin without undermining the mystery of Christ' (CCC # 389). Yet this is what is happening right throughout Australian Catholic schools. Most of the teachers refuse to believe that their own children were alienated from God on the sole basis of their being a human. However, the Original Sin motif is the basis for the dogma of the atonement, whereby Christ's mission because of the fall of Adam is to reconcile humans to God through his sacrifice on the cross. Indeed, the Church proclaims Adam's action in its Easter Liturgy as a 'happy fault' which produced such a wonderful sacrificial Jesus. The irony is, it is tentatively asserted that most Australia Catholic teachers do not teach this. Instead, it appears that they are creating an alternative Christology for the presence of Christ, which has little to do with a sacrifice for personal or corporate sin. If this conclusion can be confirmed with more extensive research, it indicates that Australian Catholic teachers are emphasizing a Christology on the basis of personal understanding and life experience, not the official Christology as taught by the Church. It appears, then, that the whole Australian Catholic school system is being served by dedicated staff members who are committed to something in so many ways different from and beyond what their employer, the institutional Church thinks they ought to be about.

Purpose of Catholic schools

The conclusion of this chapter mirrors its introduction by examining the purposes of Catholic education. Three goals of Catholic schooling that were perceived as relevant at Catholic education's Australian birth were examined. The chapter concludes by offering another three goals which may well be appropriate for twenty-first century Catholic education.

The goals have to begin with Jesus and his mission, which the Scriptures record as the 'Kingdom' (Fullenbach, 1955). This term is mentioned 123 times in the Gospels. In brief, 'Building the Kingdom' demands that the fundamental purpose of Catholic education be the undivided and focused pursuit of the enhancement of human dignity. This purpose can be expressed alternatively as the nurturing of humans to be more authentically human (Martini, 2000). This concept has been expressed in a recent Vatican document as: 'The Catholic school sets out to be a school for the human person and of the human person' (Congregation for Catholic Education, 1998). The theological underpinning for this conclusion is grounded in Jesus the human being (Wink, 2002). The following premises generate the ultimate fabric of a Catholic school.

- Humans somehow image God and this imaging is fundamental to understanding the human person.
- Since Christ is fully human, to aspire to become fully human is essentially to become more Christ-like; (this concept is important and torpedoes the dualism that still 'white ants' Catholic rhetoric and practice).
- Spirituality is a characteristic of all of humanity and therefore to become more human is to become more spiritual.
- To be fully human presupposes relational and communitarian dynamics, which demand the honouring of social justice imperatives.

From this theological framework, three core goals of authentic contemporary Australian Catholic school education emerge. Catholics schools aspire to provide: (1) an integral quality education, (2) the nurturing of human community, and (3) a liberation of forms of oppression. It is appropriate to scrutinize how these goals might be achieved.

An integral quality education

- Quality education is seen as a vehicle to enhance the individual's and community's humanity;
- A balanced and critical application of the national curricula;
- Presentation of education through the perspective of a Catholic 'world view' or anthropology and its accompanying values;
- Holistic presentation of subject disciplines, the arts and sport with the nurturing of academic, emotional and spiritual intelligences;
- The systematic, scholarly and critical exposure of students to the essentials of the Catholic tradition;
- Opportunities for private and meaningful communal prayer and worship;
- Collaboratively planned retreats or reflective experiences aimed to nurture students' and staff members' (and their spouses') spirituality.

The nurturing of human community

- A preference for the collaborative and team learning in the curriculum where appropriate;
- Extracurricular resources and activities which focus primarily on the welfare of all students;
- An organized and professionally resourced pastoral care program;
- Sharing of school resources with the lesser resourced Catholic community;
- Institutionalized structures promoting horizontal and vertical communication within the school;
- Staff professional in-service based on their own personal and students' developmental growth issues;
- Extensive and organized family educational outreach assisting positive parenting in the areas of communication, personal and vocational growth and drug education.

A liberation of forms of oppression

- A leadership that is practised as stewardship and is characterized by service devoid of self-interest, rank without privilege, justice, collaboration, transparency and accountability;
- Honest reviews conducted by ethical person/s of structures that maybe pragmatic, competitive, consumerist and materialist;
- An understanding that employment in a Catholic school entails a sense of vocation for all and for some an acceptance of a ministry;
- A curriculum and resultant structures that honour the common good over individualistic agendas;
- The systematic exposure of students to Catholic social justice teachings, especially through well-prepared, conducted and debriefed immersion programs challenging students' values;
- A privileging of Catholic social teaching expressed in enrolment, termination, discipline, financial, resource, social and celebratory policies, practices and traditions;
- Substantial outreach initiatives for the needy, poor and 'new poor' and marginalized.

The real impact of Catholicism on children's lives will be as it always has been, when dedicated professional teachers generously share their own expertise and humanity with their students.

Leaders of Catholic schools will know their stewardship is approaching genuine success when, as the prime catalysts for an authentic and rigorous holistic educational enterprise, students, parents and staff experience first and foremost the common decency, concern, fairness, care, graciousness and compassion of a very human Christ, in the school's daily conduct. In Australian contemporary society, it now seems that the reception of Christ in the least of sisters and brothers is a relevant prerequisite for a meaningful reception of Christ at Eucharist. 'The greatest presence of the risen Lord is another human being'.[2]

Notes

1. Bill Foster (ACU Education) contributed to the initial design of the questionnaire with Anna Sheehan (ACU Psychology) analyzing the data. Thirty-three per cent of the sample was male. One school was an all boys' school, while the other two were all girls' schools. One school was conducted by the local Catholic Education Office. The other two were religious institute schools. Almost 80% were Catholic.
2. The author of this quotation is the Canadian theologian Gene Laverdiere. I have lost the exact source of the quote.

Notes on contributor

Denis McLaughlin (PhD London) is an Associate Professor, School of Educational Leadership, Australian Catholic Education, Virginia, Australia.

References

Allen, J. (2000) *Cardinal Ratzinger: the Vatican's enforcer of the faith* (New York, Continuum).

Arthur, J. (1995) *The ebbing tide: policy and principles of Catholic education* (Leominster, Gracewing).

Arthur, J. (2002) Measuring Catholic school performance, paper delivered on *Faith Schools: Conflict or Consensus*, Institute of Education, University of London, 27–28 June.

Bowell, R. (2004) *The seven steps of spiritual intelligence* (London, Nicholas Brealey).

Campion, E. (1982) *Rockchoppers: growing up Catholic in Australia* (Ringwood, Penguin).

Catechism of the Catholic Church (Sydney, St Pauls).

Catholic Education Commission of Victoria (2004) *The affordability of Catholic schools in Victoria: access to Catholic schools by students from Catholic families* (Melbourne, Catholic Education Commission of Victoria).

Charlton, P. (2002, July 31) Grace under pressure, *Courier Mail*, p. 13.

Chesterton, P. & Johnston, K. (1998) *Access to Catholic schooling* (Canberra, National Catholic Education Commission, Australian Catholic University).

Congregation for Catholic Education (1998) *The Catholic school on the threshold of the third millennium* (Sydney, St Pauls).

Cozzens, D. (2000) *The changing face of priesthood* (Collegeville, Liturgical Press).

Dixon, R. (2003, July 28) Mass attendance trends among Australian Catholics: a significant challenge for the Catholic Church, *South Pacific Journal of Mission Studies*.

Dixon, R. (2004) Acceptance of key Catholic beliefs and moral teachings by generation X mass attenders, *The Australasian Catholic Record*, 81(2),.

Eagen, J. (1995) *Restoration and renewal: the church in the third millennium* (KS, Sheed & Ward).

Edmund Rice Education, Australia (2004) *The Charter: a proclamation of an authentic expression of Edmund Rice Education as applied to Catholic schools in the Edmund Rice tradition* (Melbourne, Christian Brothers).

Flynn, M. (1993) *The culture of Catholic schools* (Sydney, St Pauls).

Flynn, M. & Mok, M. (2000) *Catholic schools 2000: a longitudinal study of year 12 students in Catholic schools 1972–1982–1990–1998* (Sydney, Catholic Education Commission, NSW).

Fogarty, R. (1959) *Catholic education in Australia 1806–1950* (Melbourne, Melbourne University Press).

Fullenback, J. (1995) *The kingdom of God: the message of Jesus today* (New York, Orbis Books).

Greening, W. (1989) The adaptation of the Irish Christian Brothers' system to Australian conditions in the nineteenth century. Unpublished PhD thesis, University of Melbourne.

Gremillion, J. & Castelli, J. (1987) *The emerging parish: the Notre Dame study of Catholic life since Vatican II* (San Francisco, CA, Harper & Row).

Griffiths, W. (1999) Parental expectations of a Catholic secondary school. Unpublished EdD thesis, Australian Catholic University.

Holloway, R. (2001) *Doubts and loves: what is left of Christianity?* (Edinburgh, Canongate Books).

Hughes, J. (2003) Popular culture's new high priests, in: C. McGillion (Ed.) *A long way from Rome: why the Australian Catholic Church is in crisis* (Sydney, Allan & Unwin).

Hughes, P. (2000) *Australia's religious communities: a multimedia exploration* (Melbourne, The Christian Research Association).

Mackay, H. (1999) *Turning point: Australians choosing their futures* (Sydney, Macmillan).

Martini, C. (2000) *On the body: a contemporary theology of the human person* (Melbourne, John Garratt).

McGillion, C. (2003) Visions, revision and scandal: a church in crisis, in: C. McGillion (Ed.) *A long way from Rome: why the Australian Catholic Church is in crisis* (Sydney, Allan & Unwin).

McLaughlin, D. (2000) *The Catholic school: paradoxes and challenges* (Sydney, St Pauls).

McLaughlin, D., Begg, P., Pollard, B. & Wilkinson, D. (2005) Faith belief and practices of teachers in Catholic schools. Unpublished research, Australian Catholic University.

Mullins, M. (2003) Has the Church a future? The generational divide, in: C. McGillion (Ed.) *A long way from Rome: why the Australian Catholic Church is in crisis* (Sydney, Allan & Unwin).

National Catholic Education Commission (2000) *Australian Catholic Schools: why have them and what they aim to achieve* (Canberra, National Catholic Education Commission).

O'Donnell, D. (2001) Young Catholics surveyed, *Doctrine & Life*, 51(10).

O'Loughlin, F. (2000) *Christ present in the Eucharist* (Sydney, St Paul).

Ormerod, N. & Ormerod, T. (1995) *When ministers sin: sexual abuses in the churches* (Newtown, Millennium).

Paul VI (1982) Evangelisation in the modern world, in: A. Flannery (Ed.) *Vatican Council II: more post conciliar documents* (Dublin, Dominican Publications).

Praetz, H. (1980) *Building a school system: a sociological study of Catholic education* (Melbourne, Melbourne University Press).

Queensland Catholic Education Commission (2001) *Catholic schools for the 21st century* (Brisbane, Queensland Catholic Education Commission).

Ryan, P. & McLaughlin, D. (1999) Tensions in Australian catholic education: the dialectic of Catholic education, *Word in Life*, 47(2).

Sultmann, W., Thurgood, G. & Rasmussen, B. (2003) What parents are thinking: some reflections for choices for schooling, *Catholic School Studies*, 76(2).

Tacey, D. (2000) *Re-enchantment* (Melbourne, Harper Collins).

Tacey, D. (2003) *Spirituality revolution* (Melbourne, Harper Collins).

Tinsey, W. (1998) Teachers, clergy and Catholic schools. Unpublished doctoral dissertation, Australian Catholic University.

Turner, N. (1992) *Catholics in Australia—a social history* (Melbourne, Collins Dove).

Wink, W. (2002) *The human being: Jesus and the enigma of the Son of God* (Minneapolis, MN, Fortress Press.)

Index

Faith Schools